Peter Haggard
with Jane Monroe

REWILDING

NATIVE GARDENING FOR THE PACIFIC NORTHWEST AND NORTH COAST

The Press at Cal Poly Humboldt

I0105759

Cover design by Sarah Godlin
Editing, typesetting, and layout by Wilder Yaconelli and Sarah Godlin
Photos by Peter Haggard
ISBN: 978-1-962081-25-2
©2025 Peter Haggard and Jane Monroe
The Press at Cal Poly Humboldt
California State Polytechnic University, Humboldt
University Library
1 Harpst Street
Arcata, California 95521-8299
press@humboldt.edu
press.humboldt.edu
This book has been made available under a Creative Commons Attribution-
Non-Commercial 4.0 International (CC BY-NC 4.0). For details, please refer
to creativecommons.org/licenses/by-nc/4.0/legalcode.

Homo sapiens
"Jane Monroe"

Contents

- - - - - - - - - - - - - -

Grab Your Trowel

Think of this book as a garden tool—a trowel, perhaps—for unearthing the full potential of your garden, yard, or neighborhood park. I will share my forty-three years of experience with you as I rewilded a dry-land pasture of non-native grasses, Himalayan blackberries, and invasive cotoneaster into a thriving mixed landscape of native trees, shrubs, and herbaceous plants; fruits and vegetables; and a home for wildlife. Photos and descriptions of Pacific Northwest native plants and animals will help you see what is possible in your own yard-- whether urban, suburban, or rural--and how to achieve and maintain it.

This book is for gardeners who want to get their hands dirty as they garden with an eye toward reintroducing habitat that is good for the planet; its people; and our nonhuman neighbors, the indigenous wildlife. It's for people who want to replace bird feeders with natural food and habitat for native birds. It's for people who want to produce their own food while increasing biodiversity in their garden. It's for people who are passionate about gardening and nature, and for those who want to see native plants and animals return to urban and suburban landscapes.

My wife, Judy, and I moved to Fieldbrook, California (in the northwest corner of the state, where the Pacific Northwest climate dominates) in 1977, when we purchased a parcel of subdivided cow pasture. After we built our house, we planted two thirds of the pasture with endemic trees and shrubs. They have now grown to become a small woodland, with the shrubs offering shelter, food, and nesting habitat for local wildlife. With the help of predaceous insects and birds, we maintain the rest of the former pasture as our food garden for vegetables and fruit trees.

I started gardening with my parents before I started grade school, went on to earn a degree in Wildlife Management, and spent my career working for the Humboldt County Agricultural Commissioner's office. Judy and I wrote *Insects of the Pacific Northwest*, and I taught U.C. Extension courses on gardening, orchard management, and natural history.

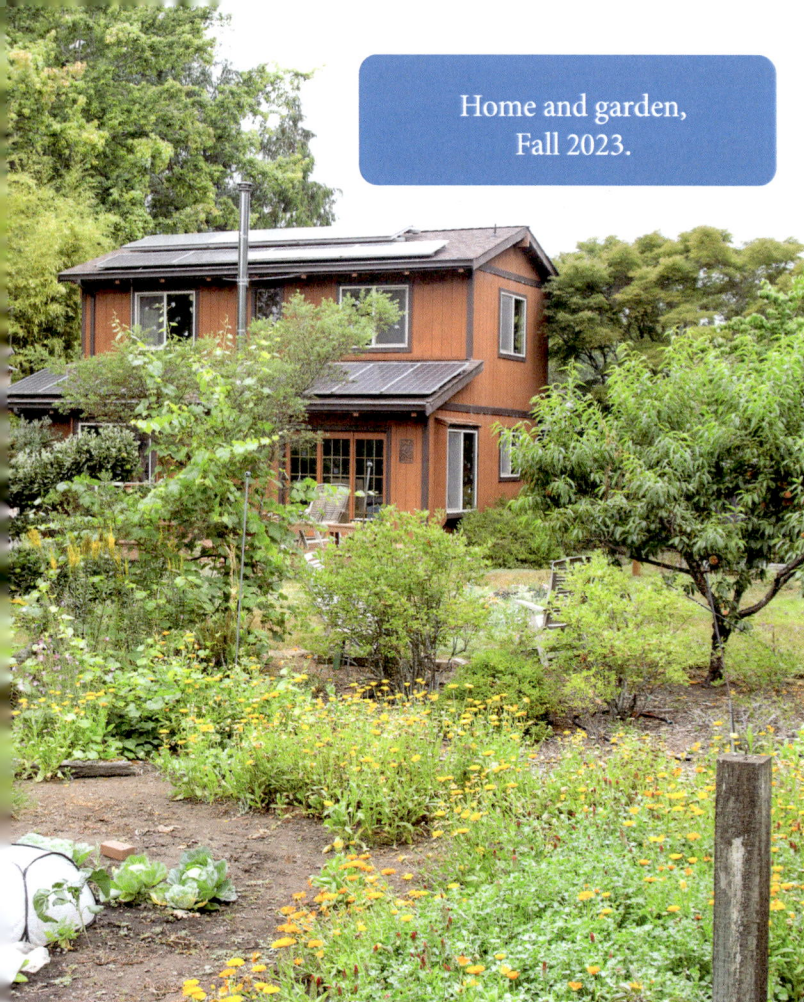

Home and garden,
Fall 2023.

and reverse the degradation of ecosystems on every continent and in every ocean." We can help accomplish that goal on a local level by rewilding our yards and neighborhoods. As the UN says, its Decade on Ecosystem Restoration "will only succeed if everyone plays a part." This book will provide you with the tools to take action and become an ethical land steward.

Grab your trowel and join me through the following chapters as we dig up a new world full of healthy, vibrant native landscapes and discover just what the night-stalking tiger beetle stalks in the night, why the woolly bear crosses the road, and why dancing

Non-native weeds and brush: red-berried cotoneaster growing alongside Eurasian forbs and grasses.

My hope is that I can provide guidance for anyone who wants to move beyond lawns, encourage and protect biodiversity, and incorporate food gardening into their native landscape.

The United Nations, concerned about the health of our planet, launched its Decade on Ecosystem Restoration on June 5, 2021, with the goal to "prevent, halt

spiders in your garden should make you want to dance too!

Life in the Urban Zone: A Green Oasis in a Wasteland of Concrete

I was born and raised in rural North Dakota and have spent most of my life in rural Northern California. I have always had a fruit and vegetable garden and been close enough to natural areas to ride a bike to these places. But for many people, especially those living in large urban areas, access to nature is difficult or even impossible. If a landscaped mall or a visit to the zoo is the closest you ever come to interacting with plants and wildlife, can you truly understand the value of biodiversity and make educated decisions on environmental issues?

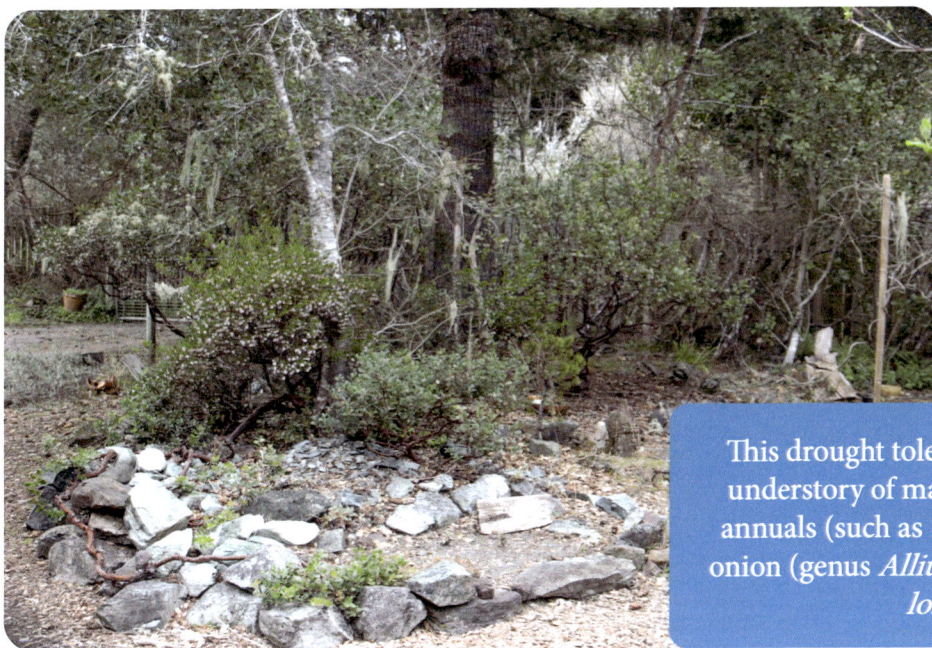

Rewilded yard with colorful native plants, including *Ceanothus thyrsiflorus*, mallow *(Sidalcea malachroides)*, monkeyflower *(Diplacus aurantiacus)*, and aster *(Symphyotrichum chilense)*.

This drought tolerant "oak woodland" supports an understory of manzanitas (genus *Arctostaphylos*), annuals (such as *Clarkia*), perennial bulbs like wild onion (genus *Allium*), and firecracker flower (*Dichelostemma ida-maia)*.

Espaliered tree: Hudson's Golden Gem apple is perhaps the finest eating russet apple.

Make new friends, such as this Pacific tree frog *(Pseudacris regilla)* guarding the winter garden from slugs.

Many cities provide community gardens for residents to grow vegetables or flowers, and garden clubs, municipal parks, adult learning schools, and native plant societies all offer opportunities to learn about nature and gardening. While these are very positive ways to enrich people's lives, they still do not enable people to have regular contact with nature. We need to provide an oasis of biodiversity in every neighborhood for the health of people and the planet.

Planted areas need to be large enough to include both plant cover and areas of exposed soil for wildlife such as bees, many other invertebrates, and small birds and reptiles. The preferred shape is generally an oval,

Pileated woodpecker *(Dryocopus pileatus)* on a red alder *(Alnus rubra)*. The tree provides the woodpecker with food and nesting space.

in order to help protect the interior from human interference. Selection of endemic plants is critical to form a balanced*, long-lived**, stable community***. Trees, shrubs, herbaceous perennials, and annuals should all be considered and the needs of native wildlife kept in mind.

    *balanced: no one plant dominates; there is a mix of different heights and leaf shapes; both evergreen and deciduous plants are included.

    **long-lived: longevity of the landscape, rather than of any one plant in particular.

    ***stable community: a community that will become more bio diverse and resilient as it matures.

    No one of us can save the world but each of us can make a difference: GARDEN!

A natural cavity in this California wax myrtle *(Morella californica)* is a source of food and shelter for a California slender salamander *(Batrachoseps attenuatus).*

Designing and Establishing 2
An Environmentally Sustainable Garden

- - - - - - - - - - - - - - -

An environmentally sustainable garden is a place where native plants and wildlife—birds, small mammals and reptiles, insects, and more—are welcome and their needs are recognized. It is a space that you create by planting native plants in your yard and providing landscape stability throughout all four seasons.

In 1983, I planted woody trees and shrubs around the edge of my property. Among the deciduous trees I planted was shining willow *(Salix lasiandra)*. Endemic to the West Coast, it grows from southern California to Alaska, along the coast and up to 2000 feet in elevation. Shining willow provides privacy and soundproofing for my home and, like all willows, it offers excellent habitat and food for wildlife all year round. Pollinators appreciate the spring flowers, and summer through fall the willows supply food for many leaf eating invertebrates. Moth larvae attracted to the willows furnish food for birds and other insectivorous animals. In winter when the branches are bare the willows' fallen leaves create shelter for overwintering invertebrates which, in turn, are exploited by hungry shrews and thrushes throughout the season.

The foundations of a wildlife garden are native or endemic plants. Native plants and wildlife often have mutually beneficial relationships. For example, as mentioned above, willows are a food source for many insects and provide shelter for nesting birds. The insects, in turn, are eaten by the nestlings, which helps control herbivory on the plant. Both willow and bird benefit from each other. Likewise, the relationship between flowers and bees (both honey bees and native bees) is critical to a healthy garden: Bees pollinate flowers while collecting pollen and nectar for food, thus ensuring another generation of flowering plants as well as food for future generations of bees.

Choosing the right plants for your garden will help kick-start these mutualistic relationships. Here, I will describe my process

Shining willow *(Salix lasiandra)* in flower.

Solitary bee in the genus *Andrena* nectaring and collecting pollen on willow flowers.

Willow leaf beetle
(*Chrysomela aeneicollis*)
eggs, adult, and larvae on
willow leaves.

Douglas' pine squirrel
(*Tamiasciurus douglasii*).

for choosing plants and establishing a
native plant landscape.

SITE EVALUATION

First, evaluate the site: soil condition,
drainage, and sun and wind exposure should all
be considered.

Soil Condition and Drainage

Most urban and suburban sites will already have plants such as lawn or ornamentals, so the soil should be good enough for native plants, which are generally less fussy. Don't overthink things like soil fertility, pH, or amount of organic material. Native plants will adapt to whatever the site gives them.

I don't incorporate organic amendments (plant or animal based additions) into my garden soil before planting, since native plants in a healthy landscape won't need it. However, if you are working with a site that has lost all its top soil or had its structure destroyed by heavy equipment, then amendments might be useful to help restore the soil's health. Composted plant material should always be your first choice. Creating your own compost from kitchen and garden scraps is a great way to ensure that your gawrden will be getting high quality organic amendments.

Inorganic amendments include vermiculite, perlite, pea gravel, and sand. Their purpose is to provide structure and improve drainage, but they should be avoided in a native garden because they can drastically change the original structure of the native soil.

Mulching is not the same thing as adding amendments to the soil. To mulch is to place a material such as compost around a plant, on the soil surface but not touching the base of the plant. The purpose of mulch is to insulate the roots, stabilize temperature and moisture levels, and enrich the soil as the mulch

White-crowned sparrow (*Zonotrichia leucophrys*) nest with eggs on willow tree.

decomposes. Because of these effects, mulching can help woody plants establish a strong root system when they are first planted in your landscape.

I rarely use fertilizers, though I do occasionally apply a foliar fertilizer, which is less wasteful and more efficient. Plants that grow slowly and steadily will have a better balance of roots to leaves than

Creating your own compost from kitchen and garden scraps is a great way to ensure that your garden will be getting high quality organic amendments.

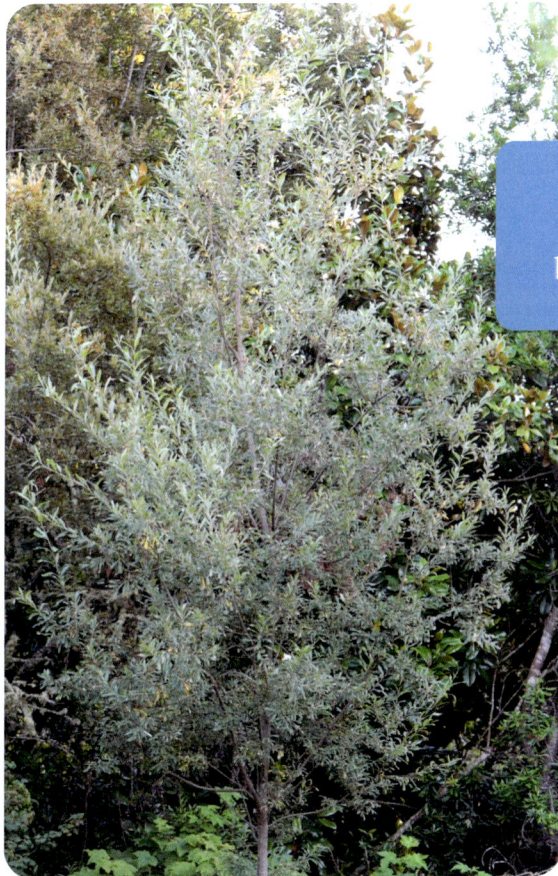

Sitka willow *(Salix sitchensis)* sporting beautiful gray leaves.

fertilized plants, and are less susceptible to diseases. Also, nitrogen—a major component of fertilizers—can end up polluting waterways and groundwater.

Soil drainage refers to the ability of water to flow through the soil. The basic rule is that good drainage suits most plants. Soil that is waterlogged or composed of heavy clay provides less air to plant roots. This can stunt the plant's growth and often causes root rot. Even plants that like wet roots, such as large-leaved lupine *(Lupinus polyphyllus)*, will not survive in water-saturated soil.

New plants, if planted in the fall after the

rain starts, should survive well on the Pacific Northwest's winter rains and need little irrigation after their first year.

Sun and Wind Exposure

The West Coast encompasses such a vast and biodiverse area that terms like "native plants" don't hold much meaning. "Endemic plants" is a far more precise phrase, indicating plants that grow only in a specific and limited area. Think "southwestern coastal Washington" rather than "Washington." Endemic plants that are obtained locally are highly recommended for wildlife landscaping, since they will be best adapted to your local climate and will be most useful to native wildlife.

When deciding what to plant, ask yourself a few questions regarding exposure. The answers to these questions will help you deter-

Biodiversity can be high even on a few inches of bark: Red alder *(Alnus rubra)* provides niches for lichens and homes for invertebrates.

mine which plants will do best in your landscape:

Is the garden going to be regularly exposed to strong winds? A strong north wind will have an impact on tender plants and, especially in the spring, on new growth. Tender or young leaves can be burned by strong, cold winds and over a period of years the shape of the plant will be altered as its north-facing growth is damaged. Planting tall, wind tolerant plants to block prevailing winds will moderate these effects. Beach pine, silktassel, and Sitka spruce are tolerant of strong winds and make excellent windbreaks.

Will the garden receive full sun all day, or only part of the day? Both winter and summer sun exposure should be considered when deciding where in the garden to place each plant. Many plants have specific needs as far as the amount of light they need, whether it is full sun, shade, or somewhere in

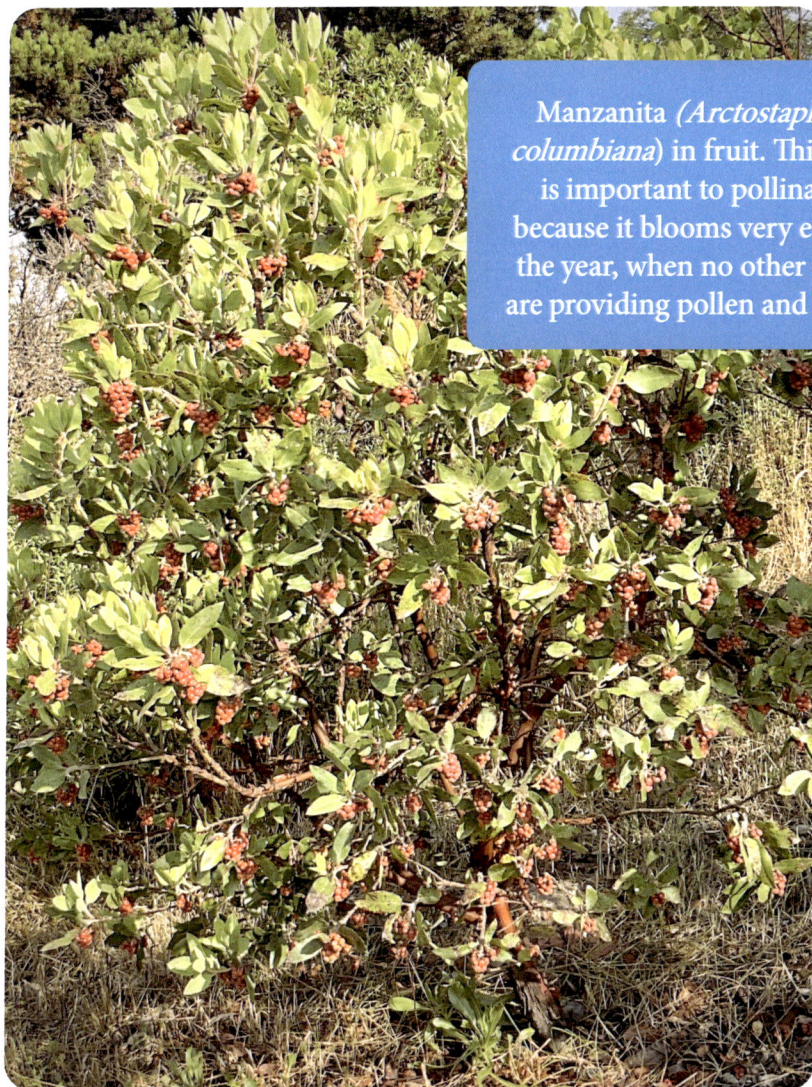

Manzanita (*Arctostaphylos columbiana*) in fruit. This plant is important to pollinators because it blooms very early in the year, when no other plants are providing pollen and nectar.

between. Be sure to assess your site's sun exposure through the seasons.

Will the garden receive frost or snow in the winter? If so, tender plants are best planted close to a south wall or under a large tree for protection from freezing weather. The USDA and Sunset have good guides to general hardiness zones, and asking at your local nursery can be even more helpful.

Remember, you want your landscape to be a reflection of what was originally there, modified by the limitations of the site and your considered judgement of what is best for the site.

Choosing Plants

Start with a list of possibilities that includes trees, shrubs, herbaceous perennials, annuals, and groundcovers. Local native plant groups and garden clubs often have such lists, and there is a suggested list at the end of this chapter—pick the plants that you find interesting and that will do well in your area. Then start looking for these species in gardens, parks, yards, or natural areas near your location to get an idea of their size, habits, and appearance when mature. While it is

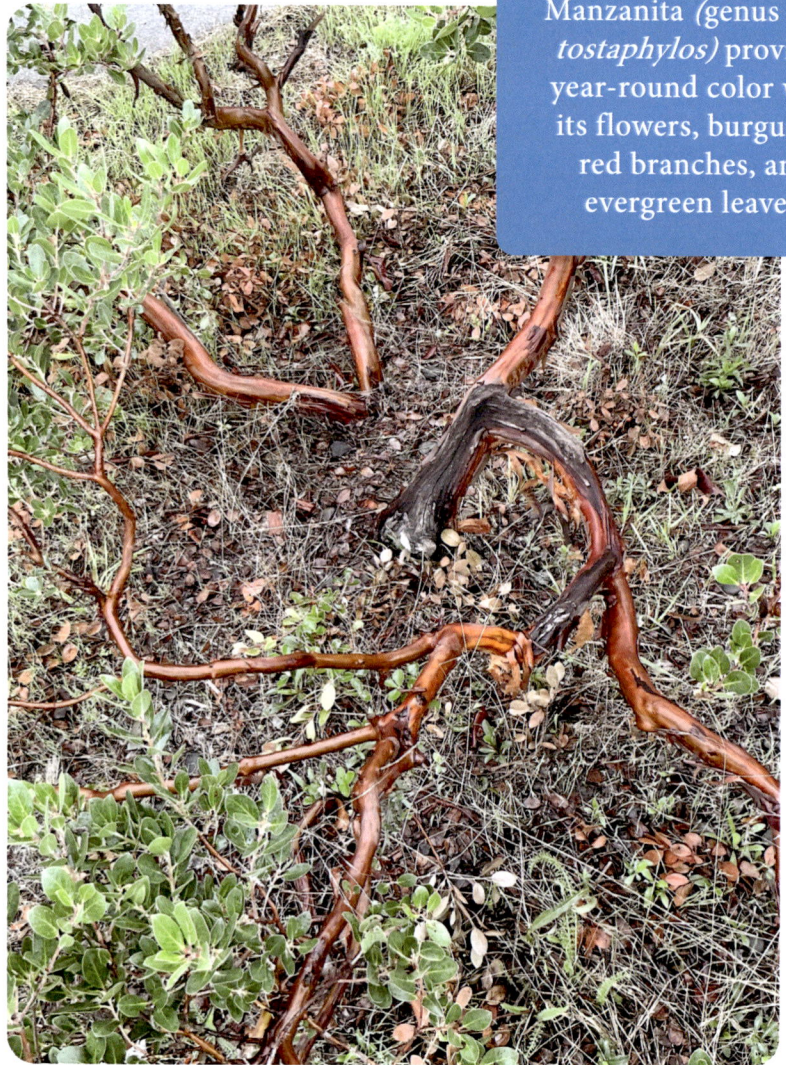

Manzanita *(genus Arctostaphylos)* provides year-round color with its flowers, burgundy red branches, and evergreen leaves.

not necessary to design the landscape before selecting the plants, a site diagram can give you a deeper understanding of your garden as well as a structured plan to follow.

With so many choices for native plants,

The flowers of *Ceanothus velutinus* (above) and *C. thyrsiflorus* (below) provide food for pollinators.

how do you decide what to put in your garden? People often seem to choose plants that they find attractive or eye-catching. Instead, ask yourself which plants the native bees and butterflies need. Always start with the insects' needs, because they are absolutely necessary for the survival of other wildlife and plants.

I have found that establishing a native landscape over several seasons is far preferable to trying to plant all the plants the first year. Start with woody plants (trees and/or shrubs), because they will form the skeleton or framework of your garden and will affect the smaller plants most directly. The shade cast by trees impacts the plants growing under and near them. Trees may also have large, aggressive roots that can outcompete smaller plants for water and nutrients. Remember that most herbaceous perennial plants and groundcovers can be dug up and moved if you are not happy with their placement (or if they are not happy with their placement!), but trees and shrubs are much more difficult—and sometimes impossible—to move successfully.

Two excellent native woody plants for birds and other wildlife are willow and alder. Alder trees are too large for a small garden, but the Pacific Northwest has plenty of willows that range in size from shrub to tree. Both alder and willow are insect magnets (a good thing!) Year-round. Even on the coldest winter day, you can find sparrows and thrushes scratching the ground under these trees looking for overwintering insects.

Most herbaceous perennial plants and groundcovers can be dug up and moved if you are not happy with their placement (or if they are not happy with their placement!)

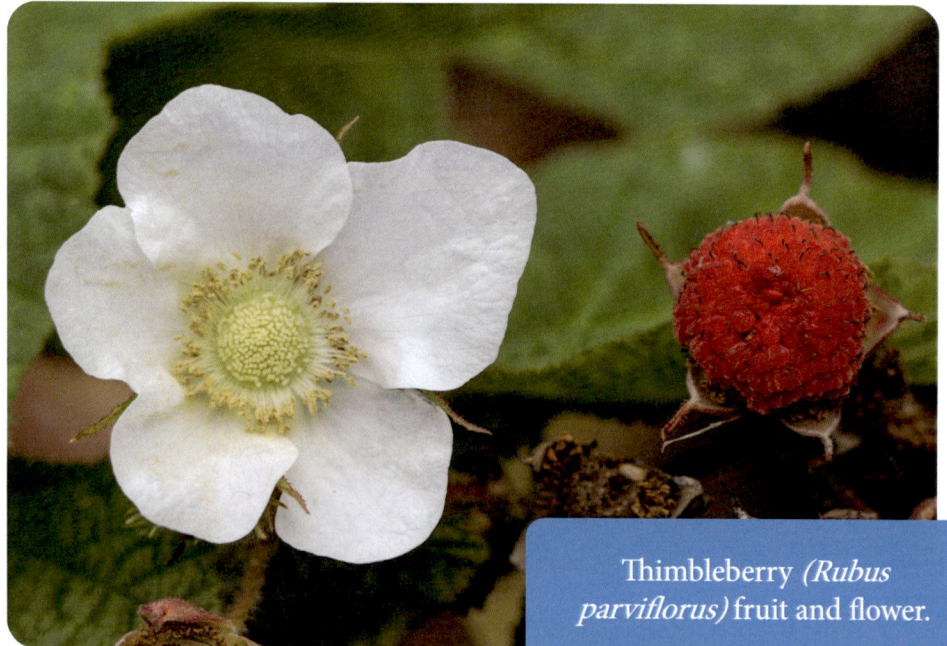

Thimbleberry *(Rubus parviflorus)* fruit and flower.

Willow thickets often provide some of the best local birding sites, and while you probably don't want to plant an entire willow thicket in your yard, one or two of them can be of great benefit to birds.

To provide a stable food source for pollinators, manzanita (genus *Arctostaphylos*) and members of the genus *Ceanothus* (such as *C. velutinus* and *C. thyrsiflorus*) are excellent choices. Manzanitas are the most important nectar and pollen producers in late winter, when bumble bee queens and hummingbirds often rely on them as their only food. *Ceanothus* is a reliable food source in the spring for pollinators and other wildlife.

Other native woody plants to consider for wildlife are thimbleberry, gooseberry, currants, and blackberry (our native species, *Rubus ursinus*, rather than the invasive Himalayan blackberry, *Rubus armeniacus*). All provide fruit

Gooseberry (genus *Ribes*) in fruit.

for birds and flowers for pollinators. Himalayan blackberry is particularly aggressive in riparian habitats, where it outcompetes groundcovers and then shades out smaller trees and shrubs. It should not be planted or encouraged to grow in any wildlife landscape.

Start Small and Think Stability

Start small. Don't try to plant the whole landscape at one time. If you plan and plant one section of your yard each year, it will be far easier to manage. Many of your new plants may need watering and weeding for their first year to help them get established, so tackling one segment per year will help you keep your plants and you healthy and happy.

As you plan and plant your landscape, an important concept to consider is stability. Even in a small plot, plants and animals will soon become a community of organisms that are dependent on one another. Frequent landscape change simplifies this environment and prevents the biological community from expanding and stabilizing over time. The end result is a loss of biodiversity.

By focusing on stability, you allow the landscape to develop gradually as the plants mature. Their leaves enrich the soil and their roots stabilize it, allowing better water penetration. The canopy provides shelter to wildlife and softens the impact of rain hitting the soil. As the native plants expand and gain strength, weeds have a more difficult time establishing themselves. Older trees in the landscape provide food for wildlife and homes for cavity nesting birds and various mammals. Even the oldest trees and shrubs, especially sick and dying ones, are important as a bountiful source of life: fungi provide nutrients by breaking down the wood, and insects in the tree become food for birds like woodpeckers.

If you are reading this chapter, hopefully you're thinking of making changes in your garden to enhance its value to wildlife. The time is right! Don't be intimidated by the lengthy "instructions" in books like this. If there are native plant sales in your area, look at the plants, talk to the people volunteering, buy a plant or two and plant them when you get home to begin your adventure. Start small! As you spend more time in the garden you will see just how much you can do to turn your yard into a nature sanctuary.

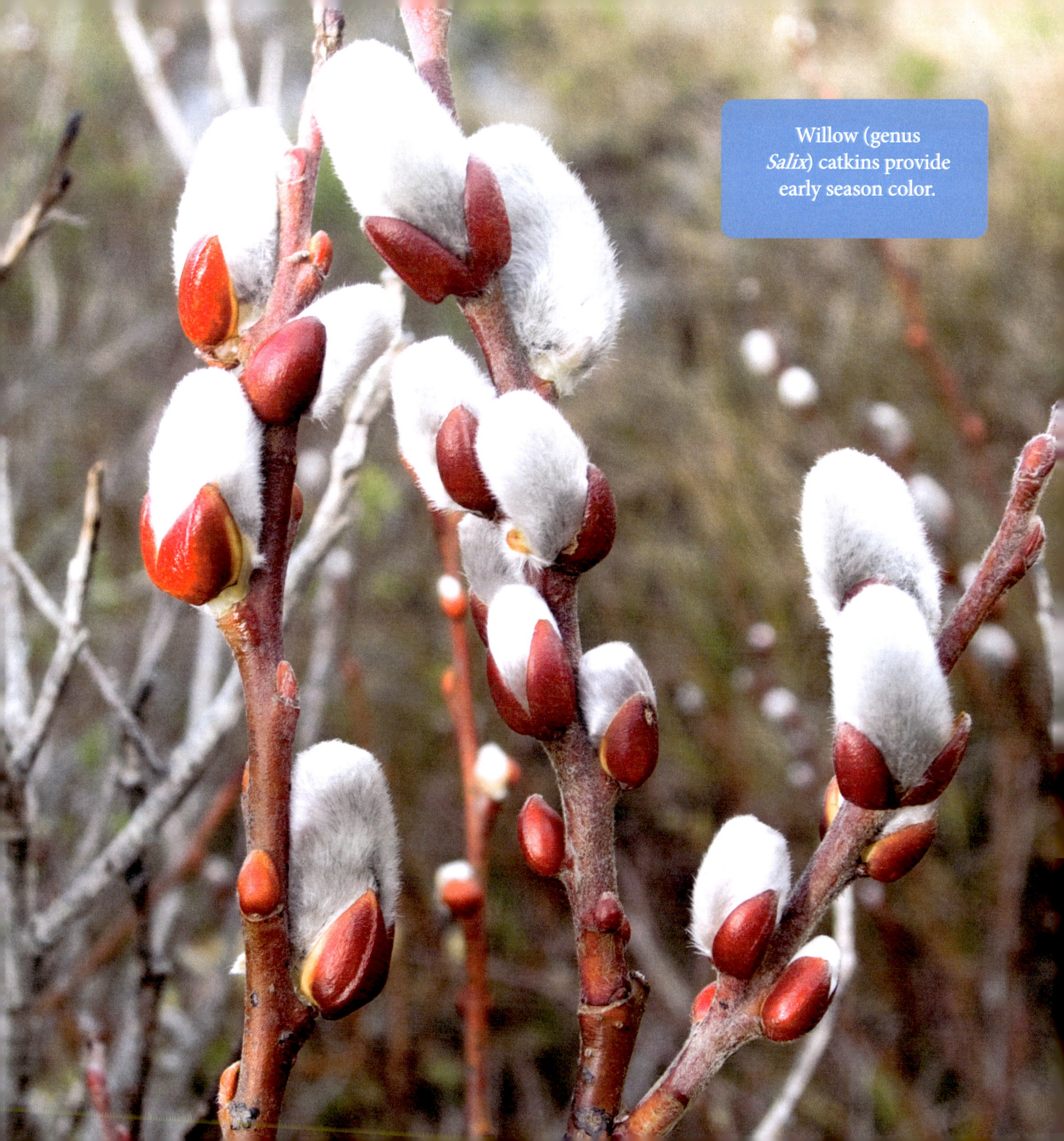

Willow (genus *Salix*) catkins provide early season color.

Pair of pileated woodpeckers (*Dryocopus pileatus*) reducing a dead alder to sawdust.

Keeping Your Allies Happy 3

When you go on a nature walk--away from neighborhoods and manicured parks--you find a much different fauna than in a typical suburban landscape. It has few of our usual garden pests, especially slugs and snails. Why? In an environment less impacted by humans, slug and snail numbers are controlled by their natural predators. Our yards, however, are simplified and disturbed landscapes: cleared of debris, watered, fertilized, and landscaped so that predators cannot survive. Natural areas are stable and provide appropriate niches for predators of pests to live, breed, and seek prey. The fresh ideas provided in this chapter will help you to provide a natural home for endemic wildlife, such as predatory carabid beetles that will be only too happy to eat slugs and snails for you.

INSECTS

One very useful component of your rewilding toolkit will be the ability to identify beneficial insects, so here I will focus specifically on the insects commonly found in a healthy backyard garden.

Ground Beetles

One of the most beneficial families of insects in the Pacific Northwest is Carabidae, the ground beetles. Most of these beetles have hardened wing covers with functional wings underneath; many are black in color, often with green or purple iridescence. The larger ground beetles frequently have fused wing covers and cannot fly. All prefer to scurry along the ground rather than fly, which makes them easy to find and observe.

Carabids in general are nocturnal and predaceous, both as larva and adult. Many can defend themselves from other predators with their large jaws, heavy exoskeletons, and noxious defensive chemicals. After handling a ground beetle, sniff your hands to see if you have been marked! These chemicals are harmless to humans, but can protect carabid beetles from insect predators.

European ground beetle attacking a slug *(Arion ater)* which has assumed a defensive posture, using slime for protection.

A common carabid in most gardens is the flightless European ground beetle *(Carabus nemoralis)*. The adult is a beautiful dark purplish or greenish bronze with copper iridescence on the edges of its thorax. While it is an opportunist, I frequently see the adult eating slugs. Pick one up to study it, and be sure to notice the foul-smelling brownish-red liquid that it regurgitates onto your fingers to defend itself. The larva of the European ground beetle, which is long and narrow and mostly black, is one of the few diurnal carabids. Find them after watering your summer garden, when they attack earthworms driven to the surface by the flood of water. This beetle species is considered synanthropic--it benefits from an association with humans. In fact, in order to survive and reproduce, it requires a habitat that we humans

Adult European ground beetle *(Carabus nemoralis)* with distinctive copper iridescence.

cultivate, plant, and weed: our gardens.

Adult and larval ground beetles tend to be opportunists, consuming any animal small enough for them to catch. However, some are specialists. The adult snail killer or snail eating carabid *(Scaphinotus angusticollis)* has a narrow, elongate head and thorax— the perfect adaptation for reaching into a snail shell to get every last bit of escargot. The snail killer is quite common in damp environments where snails or slugs abound . . . as in most vegetable gardens. Snail killers cannot

Adult snail-killer *(Scaphinotus angusticollis)*. An appealing name to a gardener!

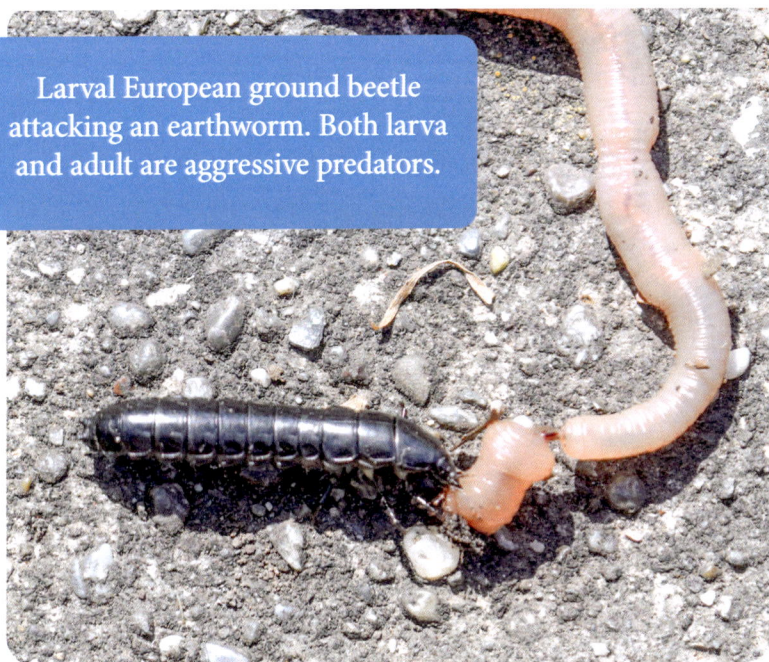

Larval European ground beetle attacking an earthworm. Both larva and adult are aggressive predators.

fly, so any you find in your garden live in it or very close by, dining on the snails that want to dine on your lettuce.

Our final carabid is another snail consumer, the intriguingly named California night-stalking tiger beetle *(Omus californicus)*. The adult California night-stalking tiger beetle is flightless, with a black body and pitted wing covers. It defends itself with a chemical that it releases from its abdomen when threatened. One of the components of this chemical defense is the almond-scented compound benzaldehyde. Benzaldehyde prevents the attacker's

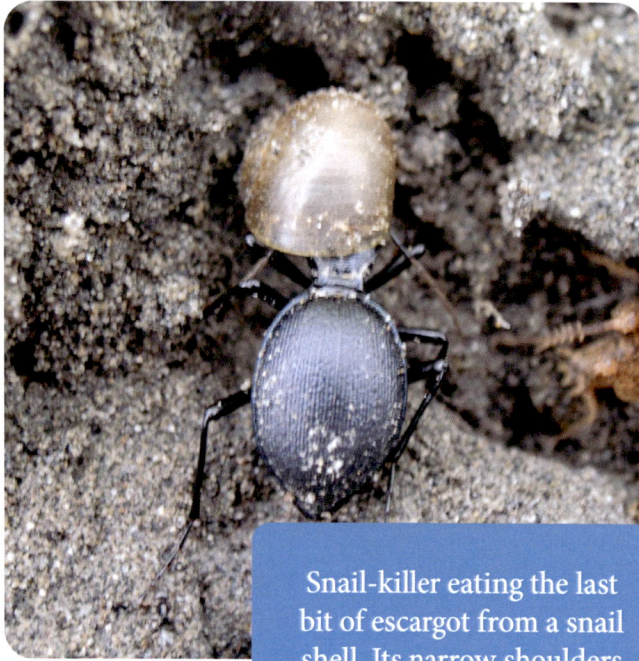

Snail-killer eating the last bit of escargot from a snail shell. Its narrow shoulders allow it to get its head and jaws inside the shell.

Glowworms are beetles, not worms, but they get the first half of their name from the fact that the adult female and the larva are bioluminescent.

antennae from functioning properly, giving the beetle more time to escape. The beetle's predaceous larva lives in a burrow for up to three years before becoming an adult. It has a pair of huge jaws and a large flat head that it uses to close the entrance to the burrow. I regularly find the adults in forested areas, but the only place I have seen active larval burrows is in my vegetable garden.

Glowworms

Glowworms are beetles, not worms, but

Adult night-stalking tiger beetle *(Omus californicus)* in winter vegetable garden.

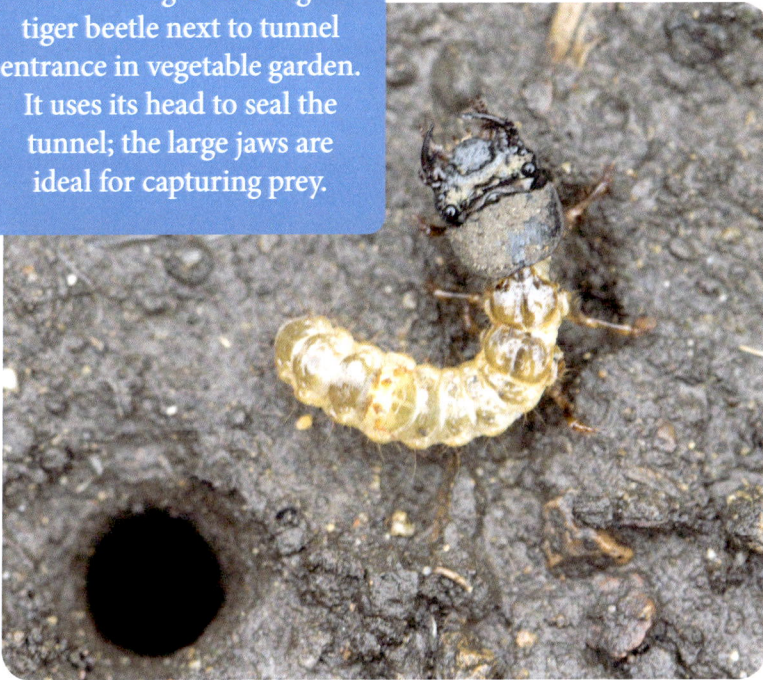

Larval night-stalking tiger beetle next to tunnel entrance in vegetable garden. It uses its head to seal the tunnel; the large jaws are ideal for capturing prey.

they get the first half of their name from the fact that the adult female and the larva are bioluminescent. This luminescence is caused by specialized light-emitting organs in the abdomen.

The common glowworm *(Pterotus obscuripennis)* is sexually dimorphic—the adult male and female have completely different body shapes, so much so that you may not realize they are the same species. The adult male has black wing covers, a red or orange thorax, big eyes, and large feathery antennae. It is recognizably a beetle, unlike the female, which strongly resembles the larva in having a long, worm-like body. Entomologists refer to these females as being neotenic: that is, they retain juvenile characteristics into adulthood.

Adult male glowworms do not feed. The larva is adapted to eating only slugs and snails, so you want to encourage them to take up residence in or near your garden. They are easiest to find when slugs are most active, during warm rains in the spring and fall/winter. In searching for them at night, I usually find the glowing larvae at the bases of plant stems.

Wasps

Wasps, especially yellow jackets, are tenacious daytime predators. There are two genera in our area, *Dolichovespula* and *Vespula*. Both are social insects. Similar to honey bees, yellow jackets have a queen and workers, but yellow jacket workers collect insects rather than nectar and pollen. The workers chew the insects into pulp and feed that to the larvae. Adult yellow jackets normally feed on liquids such as nectar.

The western yellow jacket *(Vespula pensylvanica)* is our most common yellow jacket and is normally a ground nester. Social wasps like yellow jackets and paper wasps are important predators in our vegetable gardens, constantly searching our plants for cutworms and other pests to feed to their larvae.

Stink Bugs

The spined soldier bug *(Podisus maculiventris)* is the most common predaceous stink bug in the Pacific Northwest and is active most of the summer. Stink bugs overwinter as adults; both adult and nymph are predaceous. Like other stink bugs, the spined soldier bug uses its long piercing mouthparts to inject chemicals into its prey that liquefy the internal organs. Then the stink bug consumes the fluids, leaving behind only an empty exoskeleton. It is capable of killing prey much larger than itself.

Robber Flies

The robber flies (genus

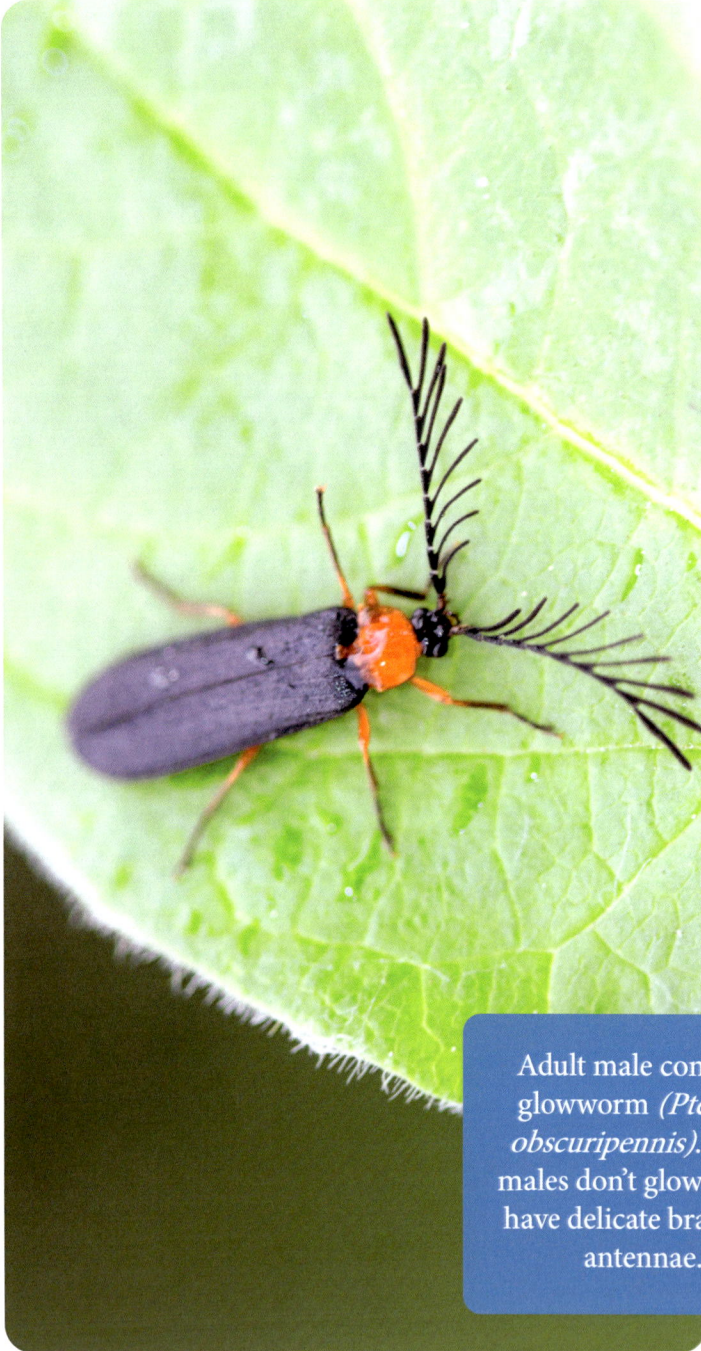

Adult male common glowworm *(Pterotus obscuripennis)*. Adult males don't glow but do have delicate branched antennae.

Laphria) are a group of colorful wasp and bee mimics. Both adult and larva are predaceous, though the adult specializes in hunting flying insects. The more colorful species in the genus seem to be more common inland, while the plainer brown species are more common in coastal areas.

OTHER ARTHROPODS

Adult female common glowworm consuming a slug. The orange tip of the abdomen glows in both females and larvae.

Centipedes

Centipedes are predaceous arthropods most often found in decaying woody debris. In the spring you can find the female centipede wrapped protectively around her large cream-colored eggs. She licks her eggs to keep them free of fungal infections. Try not to disturb her, since her offspring will help control invertebrate pests in your garden.

How to tell centipedes from millipedes? Most centipedes are flat-bodied, large-jawed, and fast moving, while most millipedes are rounder, have more legs, and coil up when disturbed. Millipedes are not

Robber flies facing off: left, *Laphria divisor*, right, *L. aktis.*

predators, preferring to dine on decaying organic material.

Spiders

Though spiders are arthropods, they are not insects. Most spiders use venom to paralyze their prey, and different species have different levels of toxins. They are excellent garden helpers, devouring pest insects that would otherwise devour your

Western yellow jacket *(Vespula pensylvanica),* our most common social wasp.

Adult spined soldier bug *(Podisus maculiventris)* feeding on a swallowtail larva.

Nymphal spined soldier bug feeding on plant-eating wasp (genus *Nematus*) larvae.

plants. There are about three thousand species of spiders in North America, but most of them are little-studied.

One common group of spiders that you are certain to notice in your garden is the orb weavers (also known as garden spiders). The female orb weavers, who are often distinctly colored or patterned, build large, roundish webs (males build smaller webs) with radiating spokes and sticky silk, precision-engineered to capture prey such as moths, flies, and the cabbage white butterfly. The web is most noticeable in the morning, when dew drops on the silk strands reflect the early sunlight and look like strings of glittering diamonds.

Orb weaver webs often span three to five feet. How does such a small creature accomplish this feat? The spider produces a long strand of silk and allows it to float in the air until it touches another surface, to which the silk sticks. With both ends of the line secure, she can now construct a scaffolding and complete her web. Most orb weavers spin a new web every day after consuming the old one, which is why their webs always seem tidy and clean.

Orb weavers are most evident in the garden in late summer and fall. The black-and-yellow

Female black-and-yellow argiope *(Argiope aurantia)* in the center of her web, her usual location.

argiope *(Argiope aurantia)* female is usually quite conspicuous in the center of her large web. The shamrock orb weaver *(Araneus trifolium)* is locally called the Halloween spider because the female is at her largest, with her abdomen full of eggs, in late October. She builds a large web, but unlike the black-and-yellow argiope, she does not stay exposed on it, rather living in an attached retreat made of silk and leaves. When she senses the vibrations of a struggling insect in her web, she immediately rushes out to subdue it. The shamrock orb weaver comes in many different colors, from brown to red to purple, but is easily identified by black and white bands on the legs.

While orb weavers are distinctive for their large webs and patterned abdomens, they are

Female shamrock orb weaver *(Araneus trifolium)* in dried-grass lair near her web.

not the only showy spiders in your garden. The crab spiders (or flower spiders) are often brightly colored and may be seen on flowers, where they sit and wait for prey such as flies and bees, with all eight legs curved forward in a crab-like fashion.

The goldenrod crab spider *(Misumena vatia)* is easily one of the most common spiders observed in the Pacific Northwest. Its yellow or white body is wide and flattened and has a red or pink splotch in the center. In the spring, look for it on apple blossoms, in summer on Queen Anne's lace, and in fall on goldenrod flowers. The female spider is able to switch body color between white and yellow so she can match her chosen flowers, but the complete change takes weeks. Male goldenrod crab spiders, which are dark brown and much smaller than the females,

Female goldenrod crab spider, white morph.

The male goldenrod crab spider looks much different than the females.

sometimes drink nectar from flowers—an unusual nutrient source among carnivorous spiders. The tiny male needs carbohydrates for energy to court females, but the female needs more proteins and other nutrients to produce healthy eggs.

Thin-legged wolf spiders (genus *Pardosa*) are extremely common in many habitats but little noticed. They are drab brown, small to medium sized, and very fast. Thin-legged wolf spiders capture their prey by pursuit rather than by snaring it in a web. The easiest place to observe them is in an unkempt lawn, where they can be very abundant. Early in the summer, look for the female dragging a white silken egg sac behind her. Once the eggs hatch, the spiderlings clamber onto her abdomen and stay there, protected by mom until they are ready to disperse.

Jumping spiders (Family Salticidae) have long front legs for grasping prey, but are most well known for their leaping abilities. They don't spin webs but use their four pairs of large eyes to locate prey, and then slowly stalk it. When close enough they swiftly jump or pounce. Being safety conscious, the jumping spider attaches a safety line of silk to the substrate and to its abdomen before it jumps. If it misses its prey and is left dangling, it simply reels in the silk to return to its original location.

Female thin-legged wolf spider (genus *Pardosa*) carrying her spiderlings.

Sometimes scientific names can tell you a lot about an organism. The zebra jumping spider is a small, common spider with black and white stripes and the scientific name *Salticus scenicus*. *Salticus* means 'dancing' in Latin, and *scenicus* translates to 'theatrical' (as in "causing a scene"). This describes the male zebra jumping spider perfectly, as he is indeed a dramatic dancer. When the male spies a female, he starts a zigzag dance involving waving his front legs and pedipalps (appendages on either side of his mouth) and moving his abdomen up and down. The female watches intently with her eight eyes. If she likes his dance moves, mating occurs. As with the thin-legged wolf spiders, the female zebra jumping spider keeps her egg sac with her at all times and then guards her spiderlings until their second molt.

OTHER INVERTEBRATES

Earthworms

Earthworm. What better name could you give to an animal that lives in the ground and

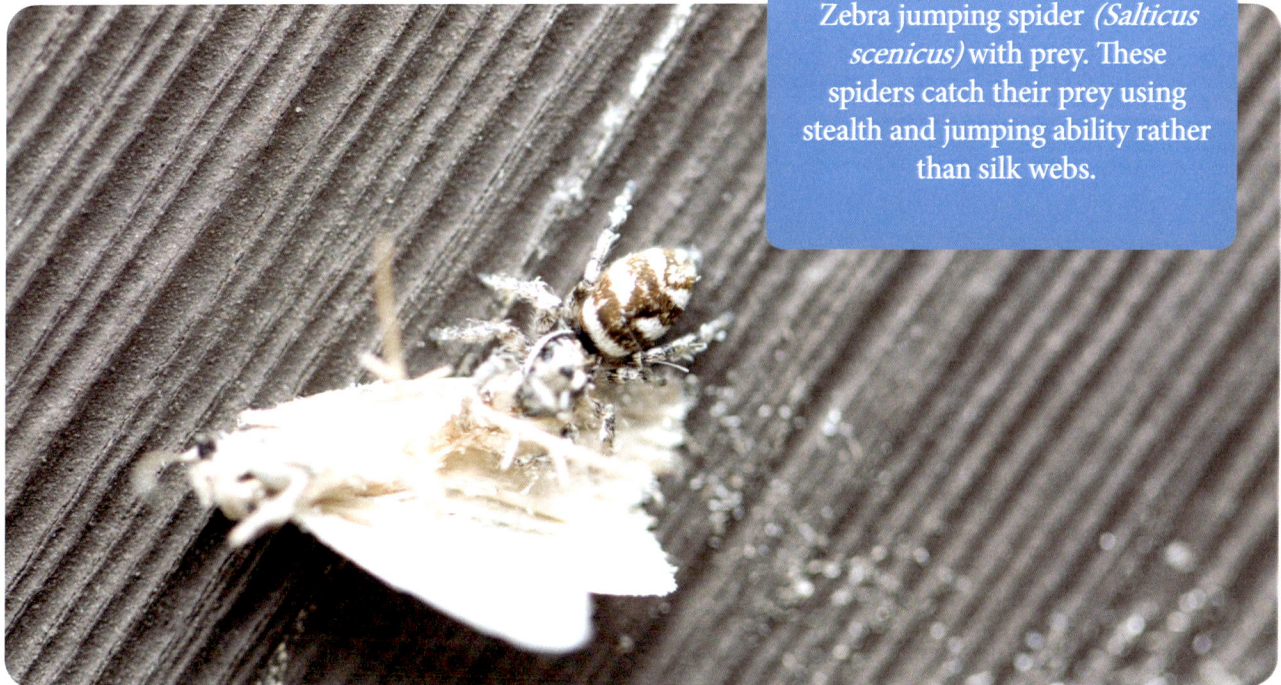

Zebra jumping spider *(Salticus scenicus)* with prey. These spiders catch their prey using stealth and jumping ability rather than silk webs.

An earthworm *(Lumbricus terrestris).* While not endemic to North America, it does play a major role in our environment.

Pacific tree frog (*Pseudacris regilla*). Males sing from late fall through winter, providing an incredible chorus at night.

builds healthy soil? The earthworm's body plan is simple: a narrow tube where earth and nutrients go in the front end, get processed in the middle, and what's left exits the back. No batteries or solar panels needed, thank you, just soil and organic debris!

The earthworm improves soil structure and fertility, helps decompose and incorporate organic matter, and improves soil aeration and drainage. Yet even gardeners give the humble earthworm little thought.

The western United States is home to approximately 28 named species of earthworm and many more undescribed species in collections waiting to be identified. One of the most common is *Lumbricus terrestris*, an introduced species from Eurasia that is now distributed worldwide. Also known as the nightcrawler, it is a large worm that lives in semi-permanent vertical tunnel systems in the soil. Nightcrawlers feed on surface litter, and make piles of soil and organic material near their tunnel entrance. They seem to be at home in a garden, especially when it is generously watered. Along with the many positive things they do for the soil, they are a very important food source for ground beetles, birds (especially American robins), toads, lizards, and shrews.

AMPHIBIANS AND REPTILES

Amphibians

All amphibians prefer moist conditions, and many live at the interface of soil and plants, often under rocks or fallen limbs where many plant pests also dwell. Amphibians are therefore our first line of defense against the eggs and immature stages of slugs, snails, and cutworms. Most of our native frogs, toads, and salamanders need permanent or seasonal water for reproduction. While this eliminates most gardens as breeding areas, we can still provide food and shelter for them. When amphibians are not breeding, they move away from water to avoid predators and seek food and shelter, and they simply need a moist place to rest during the day plus a place to find food at night—your garden.

The Pacific tree frog (*Pseudacris regilla*) is the state frog of Washington and is very common throughout the Pacific Northwest. A small "calling frog," it is usually green or brown with black eye stripes that stretch from the nose, across the eye, and to the shoulders. It has the ability to change colors in order to better camouflage itself. The change in hue is triggered by changes in air temperature and humidity as the frog moves from one environment to

Male Pacific tree frog calling; there are two egg masses nearby.

Western toad *(Anaxyrus boreas)*, warts and all.

another. Welcome this frog to your garden, since it dines on slugs and other pest invertebrates. While it is most active in the rainy winter months (its breeding season), it will remain active throughout much of the summer if it lives near a pond or well-watered garden.

The western toad *(Anaxyrus boreas)* is the most common toad in the Pacific Northwest. The adult has a very engaging personality, warts and all. If you find its home—usually under rock piles or in a hole—you can often coax it out with an insect or worm. The western toad's real value to gardeners is at night when it wanders your plot like a burly night watchman, keeping your plants safe from hungry pests like slugs, snails, crickets, and just about anything else that it can catch and swallow. Whenever a western toad adopts my garden, I feel fortunate.

Salamanders are much more physically fragile than frogs or toads, and have more exacting habitat requirements than their fellow amphibians. They require a permanently moist home with no disturbance, such as under a log or in deep organic material. Most salamanders are active in the winter after the rains have started, when

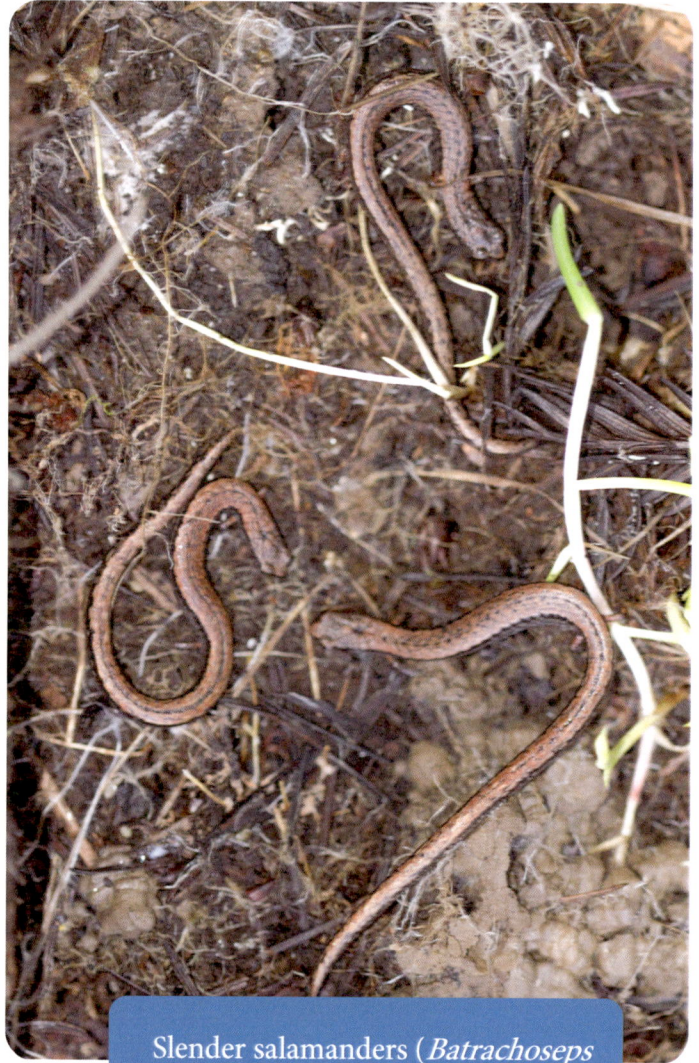

Slender salamanders (*Batrachoseps attenuatus*) may be confused with worms because of their tiny legs.

Ensatina *(Ensatina eschscholtzii)* with yellow spots at base of legs and with tail constricted at base.

slugs and snails are also busy.

Salamanders that may take up residence in your native plant garden include the slender salamander *(Batrachoseps attenuatus)* and ensatina *(Ensatina eschscholtzii)*, which don't require water for breeding. The slender salamander looks worm-like due to its narrow body, damp skin, and exceedingly tiny legs. If you look closely, you can see the four tiny toes on each foot. Ensatinas are reddish brown to dark brown above and much lighter below, with an orangish splotch at the base of each limb.

Reptiles

Fortunately for gardeners there are some helpful snakes and lizards that will readily visit our gardens. The western terrestrial garter snake *(Thamnophis elegans)* is found throughout our region and can be quite common in gardens, especially those with water features. There are many subspecies, generally dark brown in color with a distinct

Western terrestrial garter snake *(Thamnophis elegans)*. They are extremely variable in pattern and color.

dorsal stripe that is often white but sometimes yellow or pale orange. The garter snake's diet includes insects, slugs, and other small animals.

The northern alligator lizard *(Elgaria coerulea)* is common throughout the Pacific Northwest and is well-adapted to city and suburban gardens. To attract the northern alligator lizard (as well as garter snakes) to your garden, provide places for it to sun itself and breed safely. I use bricks and rockpiles with lots of niches for hiding. Invertebrates are their main diet.

Birds

The National Audubon Society and local birding societies have done a great job of educating us about birds and protecting their habitats. But I think coming from the point of view of a naturalist rather than a "birder" can provide insight into the relationship between birds and a wildlife garden.

Endemic plants are the backbone of a bird-friendly garden because they can provide the food, shelter, and nesting sites needed for a healthy bird population: directly, as fruit, nectar, and seeds; and indirectly, through the insects that feed on the native plants. In the spring and summer, fast-growing nestlings need to consume plenty of insects to be healthy. Those insects need something to eat too: native plants such as willows, ceanothus, manzanita, and more.

With old-growth forests mostly gone and old trees in urban and suburban areas scarce, some cavity-nesting bird species face hardship when it comes time to build a nest. Sapsuckers and woodpeckers excavate their own cavities in trees, but many other birds only use cavities that have already been made by another animal. You can help these species by providing nest boxes. Chickadees, nuthatches, flycatchers, wrens, American kestrels, and bluebirds can all benefit from nest boxes, though each species will require a box built to its own needs. Contact your local Audubon group or check their website to make sure your choice of nest box is actually bird-friendly. Never use a "decorative" nest box. Such boxes are made to look nice to people but are often very flimsy and are not built with the birds' needs and health in mind.

Ponds

Small ponds add visual interest to backyard gardens and can become important sources of water for wildlife (especially birds) in late summer and fall when natural areas dry out. Garden ponds also provide homes for aquatic plants, as well as breeding sites for the Pacific tree frog and many aquatic insects.

I hope you share my excitement that there is still so much of nature to be enjoyed in our backyards and neighborhood parks. Endemic plants and wildlife all have a strong will to survive and with our help they can. In return, the assistance they offer us—from enriching our lives to protecting our plants and food gardens—is invaluable. Help your garden helpers, and they will return the favor many times over!

Pair of northern alligator lizards (*Elgaria coerulea*) engaged in a mating ritual.

Cardinal meadowhawks *(Sympetrum illotum)* in mating flight. These dragonflies can successfully breed in small ponds.

Violet-green swallow *(Tachycineta thalassina)* leaving a nest box.

Red-breasted sapsuckers (*Sphyrapicus ruber*) at their nest hole in an alder snag.

Western tiger swallowtail butterfly (*Papilio rutulus*) pollinating a leopard lily (*Lilium pardalinum*).

Garden Pollinators 4

I always look forward to early spring, when the orchard blooms—a herald of the start of the gardening season. Looking out my south facing window in March and April I see three rows of flowering fruit trees and (fingers crossed) the arrival of pollinators. While I have never maintained honey bee colonies, honey bees have pollinated my fruit trees for more than forty years. They have always had help from bumble bees, orchard bees, and other native bees, plus an assortment of other pollinators such as flies, wasps, and butterflies. When I first moved to this site, it was an abandoned pasture with mostly Eurasian annual and perennial grasses but very few flowers suitable for pollinators. After approximately ten years the orchard that I planted became well-established, producing lots of flowers every spring.

Mason (orchard) bee (genus *Osmia*) pollinating an apple blossom.

When the fruit trees got bigger, the ensuing stability of the orchard and its flowers (reliable sources of pollen and nectar) allowed orchard bees and bumble bees to establish and maintain permanent populations. As I began removing weeds and planting native plants, other native bee species joined the mix.

It's helpful to divide pollinators into three categories: European honey bees *(Apis mellifera)*, native bees, and all other pollinators. The honey bee is originally from Eurasia and was introduced to North America in 1622. Honey bees are social animals and live in large perennial colonies consisting of one queen, many female workers, and at times male drones. Until recently, honey bees were the only bees given credit for most plant pollination, while native bees (those endemic to North America) were surprisingly overlooked. That changed in the late 1980s when honey bees began to suffer from several serious problems: new viral, fungal, and bacterial diseases; parasitic mite infestations; powerful new non-selective insecticides such as

Native solitary bees in their nest entrances.

neonicotinoids; and more recently, colony collapse disorder. The decline in honey bee numbers triggered scientists and commercial beekeepers to start looking at native bees as an adjunct to the honey bee.

Fortunately for native bees, scientists are studying their critical role in pollinating commercial crops and their intrinsic ecological value. These studies have also highlighted the value of hedgerows. Historically, hedgerows were simply borders of wild shrubs and trees, typically lining a field or along a road. Many hedgerows in the United Kingdom and Ireland are estimated to be more than seven hundred years old. Modern hedgerows help prevent soil erosion and, planted with native plants (shrubs, perennials, and annuals) bordering a crop, they provide food and shelter to pollinators that can help supplement the pollination done by honey bees.

What hedgerows do for agricultural areas, wildlife gardens will do for urban and suburban areas. It is simply a matter of knowing what native bees need: like all wildlife, they require food and a stable place to reproduce.

Native solitary bee species have no queen or workers. A mated female builds her nest in the ground. She excavates a tunnel with

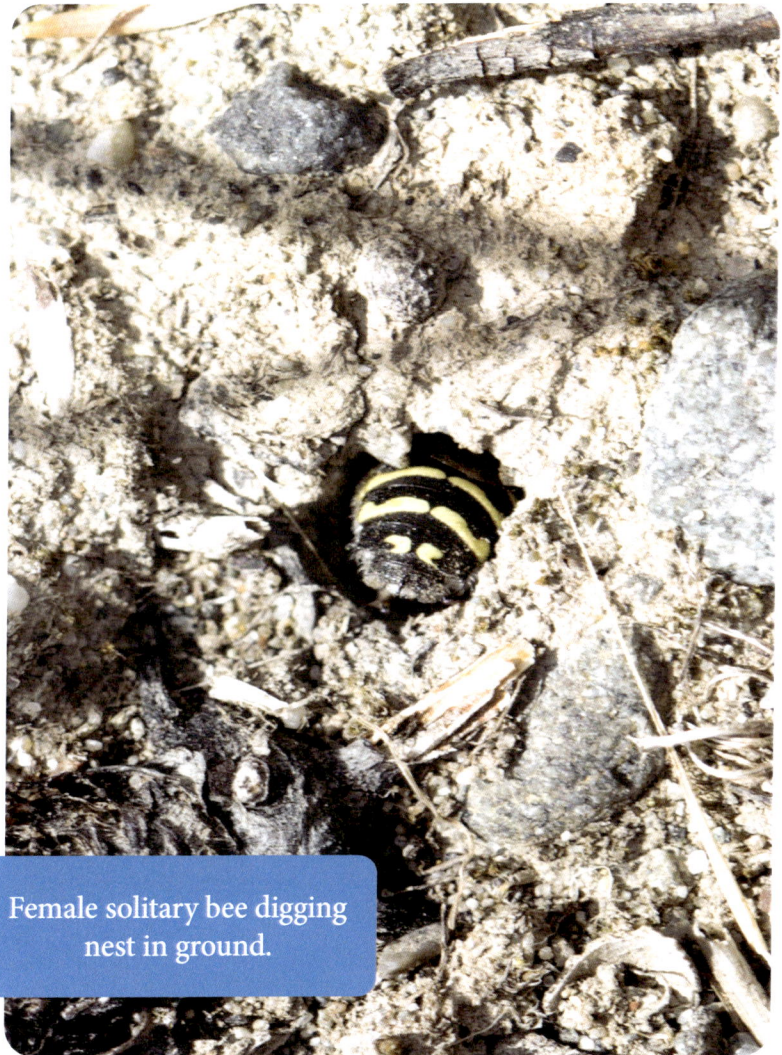

Female solitary bee digging nest in ground.

multiple cells, provisions the cells with pollen and nectar, lays one egg in each cell, and then seals the cell and eventually the nest. She provides no other parental care for the egg or developing larva. While ground nesting bees are the most common type of solitary bee, some native bees also excavate dead plant stems or use existing tunnels in wood.

Confluent-miner bee (genus *Panurginus*). Look for males early in the spring, resting on vegetation near the previous year's aggregation site or patrolling for females near nesting sites.

Mining bee (genus *Andrena*) on willow flower.

Why are native bees uncommon in urban and suburban areas? Suburban areas often have plenty of flowers to supply pollen and nectar, but they usually don't have the stable substrate that native bees require for nesting. Pampered lawns that are watered, fertilized, and mowed; or ornamentals with landscape fabric or a thick layer of bark around their bases are unusable for most ground nesting bees. They need areas of partially bare, undisturbed soil in which they can dig a tunnel and build and maintain a nest.

You may see a particular species of solitary bee collecting pollen and nectar for only three or four weeks out of the year, but the nest with eggs or larvae is there, underground, for the whole year until the adults emerge and start the cycle again.

If the soil in the nesting area is disturbed at any time of year, it can have a negative impact on the nest. The answer? Stability. Keep a small corner of your yard bare and let the bees dig their nests undisturbed.

The PNW's most common bumble bee is the yellow-faced bumble bee *(Bombus vosnesenskii)*, seen here on wild buckwheat flowers.

common mining bee genus in my wildlife garden. At least four species nest there, while many more are visitors. They are active from late winter to at least midsummer and are the first solitary bees of the year on willow blossoms.

Family Apidae—Honey Bees, Bumble Bees, and Kin

Apidae is another large family of bees. It includes the honey bees and bumble bees

NATIVE BEES

Family Andrenidae—the Mining Bees

Andrenidae, the mining bees, is the largest bee family. Small to medium-sized bees, they are clothed in many colors and patterns. All mining bees nest in the ground. They waterproof their nests with glandular secretions to protect their eggs and larvae from moisture and infections.

Andrena is by far the most

Color differences in black-tail bumble bees *(Bombus melanopygus)*: with black on abdomen (above left), and with orange on abdomen (Below).

Sitka bumble bee *(Bombus sitkensis)* male collecting nectar on California poppy.

as well as many solitary species and most of the parasitoid bees (parasitoids are parasites that kill their host). While members of this family can be small or very large, they average larger in size than other bee families. They are usually stout and noticeably hairy. The female's rear legs are covered with dense hairs for collecting and transporting pollen.

While most native bees are solitary, there is one well-known group of native social bees,

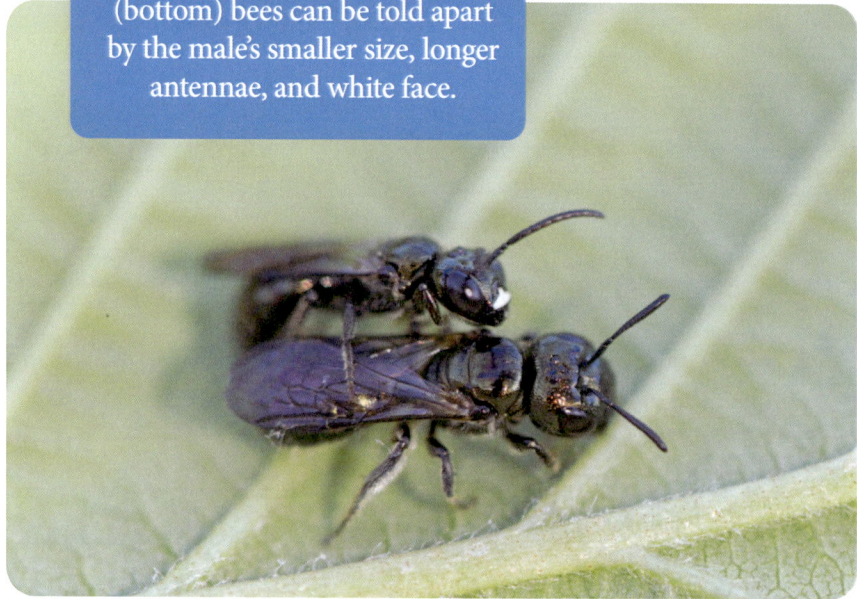

Prickly ceratina *(Ceratina acantha)* male (top) and female (bottom) bees can be told apart by the male's smaller size, longer antennae, and white face.

the bumble bees (genus *Bombus*). Large, yellow and black, and fuzzy, bumble bees live in colonies composed of a queen and her female workers. The colonies are annual, unlike honey bee colonies, and die at the end of a year. Young, newly fertilized queens overwinter and start new colonies the following

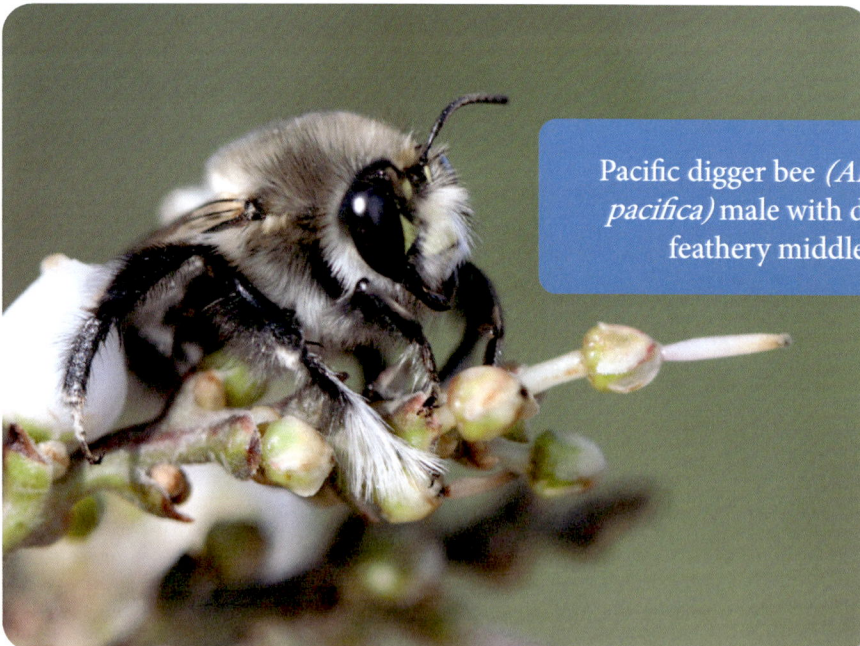

Pacific digger bee *(Anthophora pacifica)* male with distinctive feathery middle leg.

Mixed bumble bee *(Bombus mixtus)* worker entering nest; note her red-tipped abdomen.

spring. Bumble bees normally nest in the ground, though they can't dig their own nests. Instead, they must rely on abandoned runways and holes made by gophers and other rodents. Approximately thirty species of bumble bee are native to the Pacific Northwest.

The Pacific digger bee *(Anthophora pacifica)* is a large black and gray bee, and the largest solitary ground nesting bee that I have in my garden. The male has a distinct yellow face, and long brushes of hairs on the tips of his middle legs. Look for this handsome species early in the spring on manzanita (genus *Arctostaphylos*) flowers.

Prickly ceratina *(Ceratina acantha)* is the most commonly observed species of small carpenter bee in the Pacific Northwest. They have an iridescent blackish or bluish-green body with conspicuous hairs. The male has a white face and a distinctive tooth on his hind femurs. The female nests in plant stems and is very common in gardens.

Pruinose squash bee *(Peponapis pruinosa)* male waiting patiently inside squash blossom for female.

Two color forms of nomad bees (red and black bee, yellow and black bee). Nomad bees (genus *Nomada*) are kleptoparasitic. You may find the females nectaring at flowers, but more commonly they are flying near ground level searching for nests of other bees in which to lay their own eggs.

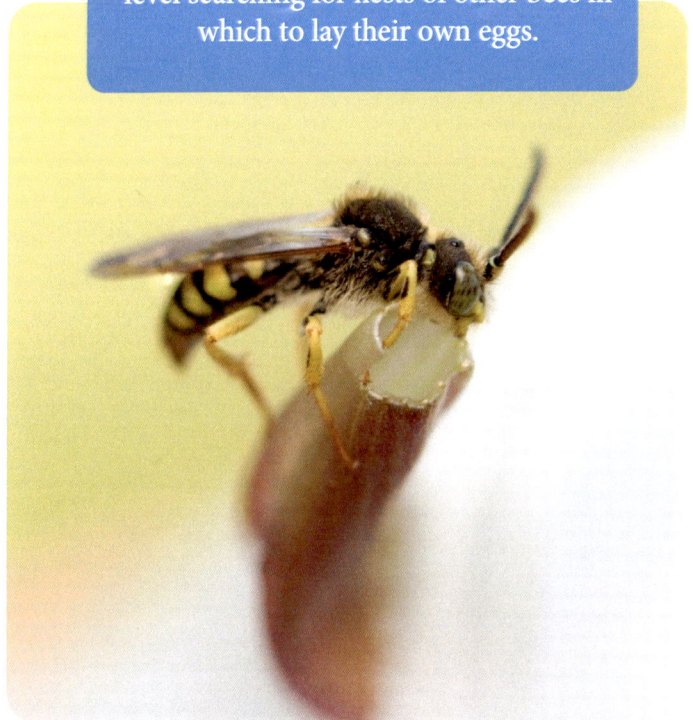

The pruinose squash bee *(Peponapis pruinosa)* is a medium-sized black bee with a banded black-and-white abdomen. The male has a small yellow spot on his face. He sleeps overnight inside squash blossoms, waiting for the flowers to open in the morning so that he can greet the females when they visit to gather pollen. Squash bees are only found in gardens where summer or winter squash are growing.

Family Colletidae—the Plasterer Bees

The cellophane bees (genus *Colletes*) are medium-sized with a moderately flattened body. Their common name comes from

Long-horned bee (genus *Melissodes*) female on wild buckwheat. *Melissodes* can be found in mid to late summer when sunflowers and related plants are blooming.

Texas striped sweat bee *(Agapostemon texanus)* female (left) and male (right).

the fact that the female lines her brood cells with a polyester coating to repel moisture (she also adds a fungicide/bactericide to the cell to further protect the developing larva).

Family Halictidae—the Sweat Bees

The sweat bees are small to medium-sized, and usually dark-colored and iridescent. The Texas striped sweat bee *(Agapostemon texanus)* is a very common bee, medium in size with a brilliant iridescent green body. The male has a black-and-yellow striped abdomen.

Females are solitary nesters but often share a single communal nest entrance in the ground. In my garden they seem to be most common in midsummer into fall, on California aster *(Symphyotrichum chilense)* and California goldenrod *(Solidago velutina* ssp. *californica)* flowers.

The tripartite furrow bee *(Halictus tripartitus)* is small and black with a faint iridescent green sheen. This bee is semi-eusocial and is one of the most common sweat bees in Pacific Northwest gardens where soil conditions are adequate and stable. Look for females provisioning their ground nests from spring to fall.

The most speciose genus of bees is *Lasioglossum*. It is a group of slender, small to medium-sized bees that are dusky black to brown with green or blue iridescence. They are extremely hard to identify to species.

Family Megachilidae—the Mason Bees and Leafcutter Bees

The mason bees and leafcutter bees differ from other families in having their pollen-carrying structure on the ventral surface of the abdomen rather than on the back legs.

The leafcutter bee (genus *Megachile*) is a medium-sized black bee with a white-banded hairy abdomen. The males of some species in this genus have pale, enlarged front legs with odor glands and a fringe of hairs resembling a hairy cup. These features are used during mating, when the male partially covers the female's eyes with his fringed legs and orients the odor glands close to her eyes and antennae.

The orchard or mason bees (genus *Osmia*)

Cellophane bee (genus *Colletes*).

Distinctly patterned cuckoo bee in the genus *Triepeolus*, a common kleptoparasite on *Melissodes*.

are stout, small to medium-sized bees, frequently iridescent green or blue in color. Look for them in early spring on flowering fruit trees and randomly throughout the summer on various flowers. I also regularly see them nesting in deep holes in redwood fence posts in my yard.

OTHER GARDEN POLLINATORS

Order Hymenoptera—the Wasps

Wasps share the order Hymenoptera with bees and ants. Many species of adult wasps visit flowers, either to consume nectar or to catch other insects for food. In the process, the wasps become significant pollinators of flowers. Walk through a flower garden in late summer or early fall and you will find both large and small wasps in many different colors and shapes.

In the Pacific Northwest the western yellowjacket *(Vespula pensylvanica)* is often the most common social wasp. Western yellow jackets are similar in size to honey bees but are not hairy and have a more sharply patterned yellow (as opposed to golden) and black body. A typical yellow jacket behavior pattern is to land on a flower to take a quick drink of nectar, check the flower for prey, then fly to the next flower and repeat the process, returning to the home nest (made of "paper") only when she has captured prey. This constant attention to flowers--especially of the carrot family--makes them important pollinators.

Order Diptera—the Flies

Flies are the first insects to "fly" in early spring and the last to fly in late fall. Look for them on willow flowers in the spring. In the fall, they can be found on various

Tripartite furrow bee *(Halictus tripartitus)* female.

Western carpenter bee *(Xylocopa californica)* male (top) and female (bottom). The female uses her jaws to carve a tunnel in wood for nesting.

Sweat bee, also known as a peacock bee *(Lasioglossum pavonotum)*.

Blood bee (genus *Sphecodes*). Blood bees are kleptoparasites that can be found where other sweat bees nest.

late-flowering plants, including coyote bush *(Baccharis pilularis)* and aster (genus *Symphyotrichum*). Flies will exploit any flowers that are open. They have no specialized body parts for collecting pollen or nectar but they do have six busy legs that get thoroughly dusted with pollen as they walk all over flowers when seeking nectar. The next time you bite into a piece of chocolate, thank a fly! They are the sole pollinators of cacao.

Family Syrphidae—the Flower Flies

One fly family that is especially attracted to flowers and is an important pollinator is the very common and aptly named flower fly. The flower fly is a bee and wasp mimic with a yellow and black body, which probably provides protection from predators. While flower flies are easy to find throughout the growing season, they become exceptionally

Leafcutter bee (genus *Megachile*) on buckwheat flower.

Painted lady butterfly *(Vanessa cardui)* nectaring on apple blossom.

Orchard bee (genus *Osmia*) on apple blossom.

common in the fall when it seems that every flowering plant has them. Their larvae are often predatory, living within aphid colonies and feeding on them.

Order Lepidoptera—the Butterflies and the Moths

Butterflies are the day-flying, showy members of Order Lepidoptera, while moths are often night-flying, smaller, and mousy brown in color. The two couldn't be more different but they are both important pollinators. Four common pollinating lepidopterans in the Pacific Northwest are the painted lady, the western tiger swallowtail, the field crescent, and the white-lined sphinx.

Starting in early spring the painted lady butterfly *(Vanessa cardui)* becomes very common in the Pacific Northwest with its annual trek north from Mexico and Southern California. The painted lady tends to fly low and fast, stopping only for nectar and to lay eggs on larval food plants such as thistles. If you have ever experienced this mass migration of thousands of northward-bound butterflies through your garden, you have witnessed a natural

Western tiger swallowtail butterfly *(Papilio rutulus)* nectaring on lupine flowers.

phenomenon that has evolved over millennia yet is becoming increasingly rare because of habitat loss.

The western tiger swallowtail *(Papilio rutulus)* is a large yellow and black butterfly common throughout the Pacific Northwest, even in urban areas. For me this is the "poster butterfly": large, easily identified, a great pollinator, and at home in both wild lands and urban areas. The adult doesn't stray far from its larval food plant—usually willows.

However, like most adult butterflies, it takes nectar from a wide range of flowers. The field crescent *(Phyciodes pulchella)* is a medium sized butterfly whose caterpillars are dependent on *Symphyotrichum* plants for food. If you have a patch of native asters, you can attract this beautiful checkered butterfly to your garden. Because the field crescent produces multiple generations in one year, you may see the adults flying from early spring to late fall.

A striking visitor to any garden is the

European paper wasp *(Polistes dominula)* nectaring on a flower.

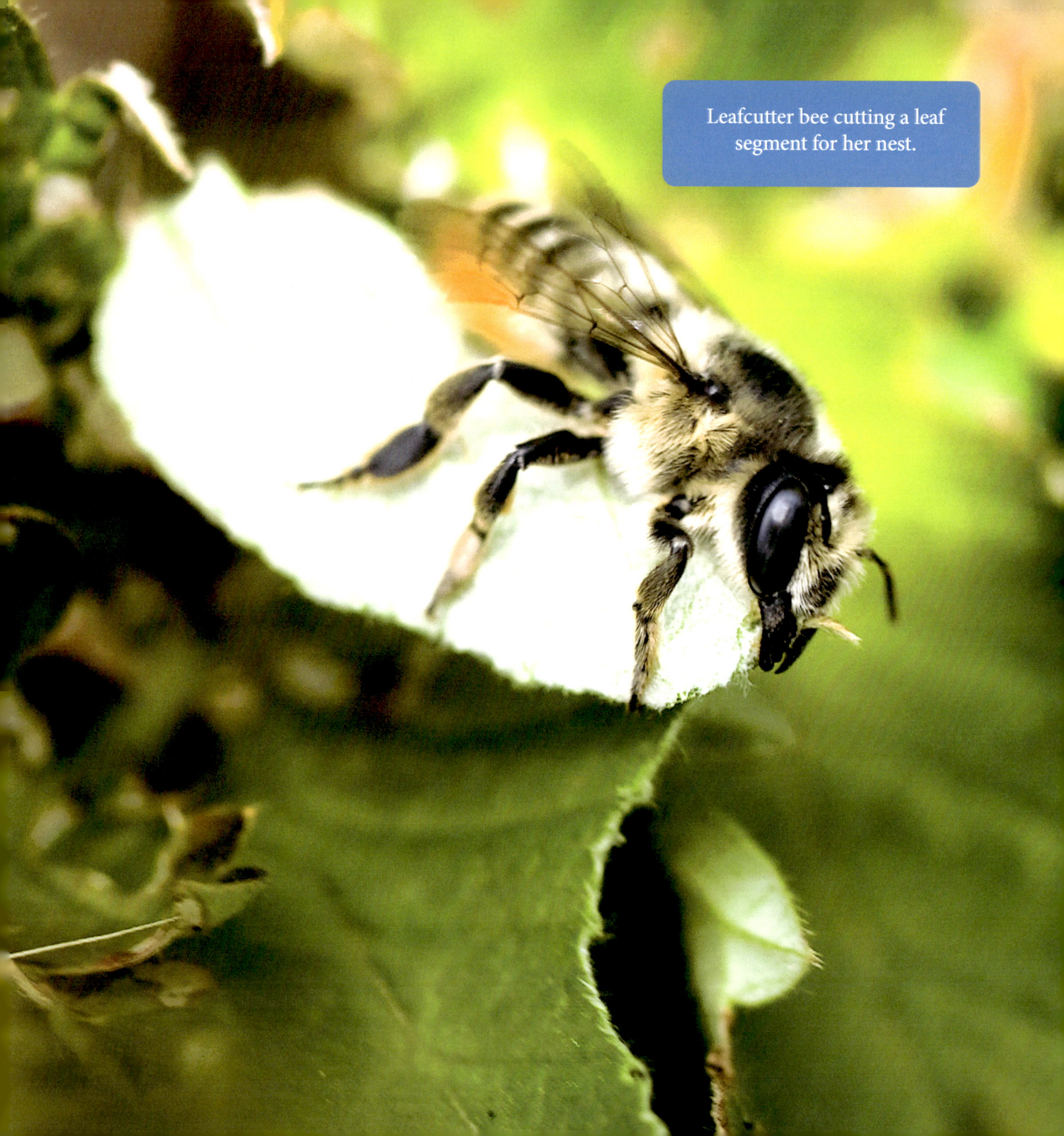
Leafcutter bee cutting a leaf segment for her nest.

white-lined sphinx moth *(Hyles lineata)*, which is sometimes mistaken for a hummingbird because of its large size and rapid wing-beats. While the three butterflies above can be seen feeding on a wide variety of flowers, the white-lined sphinx is a specialist on plants that have long tubular flowers. Due to its long tongue, it can reach nectar that bees and other pollinators can't. The white-lined sphinx prefers night-blooming flowers, but you can also find it in the early morning or evening nectaring on western columbine *(Aquilegia formosa)* and native honeysuckles such as orange honeysuckle *(Lonicera ciliosa)*.

Order Coleoptera—the Beetles

More than ten families of beetles are known to pollinate flowering plants in western North America. Two of these families are

White-lined sphinx moth *(Hyles lineata)* resting during the day.

commonly found in native plant gardens: long-horned beetles (family Cerambycidae) and soft-winged flower beetles (family Melyridae). Soft-winged flower beetles and some long-horned beetles are densely hairy. The hairs pick up and hold on to pollen, helping move it to other flowers.

Both beetle families visit many species of flowers to eat pollen and find a mate, but they are common on buckwheat (genus *Eriogonum*) and wild carrot (family Apiaceae, especially the genera *Angelica* and *Lomatium*). In the vegetable garden, look for these pollinating beetles on cilantro.

Non-insect Garden Pollinators

Hummingbirds

There is a healthy and environmentally friendly alternative to the red-dyed sugar water used in hummingbird feeders . . . it's called flower nectar!

Watch hummingbirds zip from flower to flower in the garden looking for nectar and

Flower fly *(Helophilus fasciatus)* on aster flower.

Leaf-cutting cuckoo bee (*Coelioxys rufitarsis*), aka the sharp-tailed bee. Look for this kleptoparasitic bee wherever leafcutter bees are nesting.

insects. As a hummingbird pokes its long bill and tongue into a tubular flower, it bumps its forehead into the stamens and pistil, resulting in pollen collecting on the bird's head. The next flower it visits gets the same treatment and a helping of pollen.

While honey bees are still our most important pollinators of vegetables, fruit trees,

Field crescent butterfly *(Phyciodes pulchella)* mating pair (female is larger than male).

Elderberry longhorn beetle
(Desmocerus aureipennis).

and commercial crops, pollinators such as native bees, wasps, and hummingbirds play a significant supportive role. They are also critical to the health of natural ecosystems. Because most native pollinators live, breed, and pollinate in our yards and local neighborhoods, we can and should provide safe havens for them. Use this chapter well and you will be able to create your own pollinator refuge!

Anna's hummingbird *(Calypte anna)* nectaring on manzanita flowers, one of the few nectar sources available in late winter.

Western spotted cucumber beetle
(*Diabrotica undecimpunctata*).

GARDEN COMPETITORS: WHOSE GARDEN IS THIS, ANYWAY?

5

Many of our current food and ornamental plants were brought to North America from Eurasia by European colonists, and along with the "good" plants came garden weeds, diseases, and invertebrate pests. Cole plant pests such as cabbage aphid, cabbage root maggot, and European cabbage white butterfly all came from Europe, as did all of our serious snail and slug pests.

INSECTS

Plant-Eating Beetles

While many beetles are helpful in the garden (see Chapter 3), others are not. The crucifer flea beetle (*Phyllotreta cruciferae*) is especially damaging to young garden plants in the spring and early summer.

The adult crucifer flea beetle is very small and black with a shiny bluish-green patina and enlarged hind femurs. It gets its name from its habit of springing flea-like from host plants when

Crucifer flea beetles (*Phyllotreta cruciferae*) feeding on cole plant.

threatened. Numerous small holes in a plant's leaves are a sure sign that adult flea beetles have been dining on them. The larva, which is tiny and pale yellow to white, feeds on roots and is found underground near the host plants. Infestations of larvae can kill seedlings and stunt the growth of older plants.

In the spring when adult flea beetles are feeding, damage to cole seedlings can be very extensive. Prophylactically protecting the exposed leaf surfaces with insecticides such as pyrethroids is effective, but pyrethrin is a non-selective poison and you risk killing helpful insects as well. I have not found insecticidal soaps to be useful either. Row covers, however, are very effective at preventing beetles from reaching the plants. Crop rotation is critical in order to ensure that the planting ground is

Black cutworm *(Agrotis ipsilon)* adult moth.

free of flea beetle pupae before putting the row covers on.

Two other beetle species with larvae that live in the ground and feed on plant roots are the western spotted cucumber beetle *(Diabrotica undecimpunctata)* and the western striped cucumber beetle *(Acalymma trivittatum).* The adults of both species have a green thorax with greenish-yellow wing covers, the former with black spots and the latter with yellow and black stripes.

The western striped cucumber beetle has a preference for cucurbits, but the western spotted cucumber beetle uses a huge range of host plants, including squash, corn, beans, and the tender leaves of many other vegetables. In coastal areas with mild winters, the spotted beetle is active much of the year. Adult and larva can be extremely common in the vegetable garden, where they both cause damage to young plants. Crop rotation and hand-picking the adults year-round are effective, environmentally friendly ways to keep serious damage to a minimum.

Black cutworm larva and damaged cabbage plant.

Large yellow underwing moth
(Noctua pronuba) adult.

Large yellow underwing moth pupa and larva.

While any garden can and will have other destructive beetles, in most years no controls will be necessary to prevent serious damage. I have highlighted the above beetles because they are the usual suspects that show up every year to feed on my vegetables.

Caterpillars

Caterpillars that cause trouble in the garden are the larvae of several moth species, often called 'cutworms' and 'armyworms.' While slugs and snails may be the worst pests in most gardens, cutworms are a close second.

When I discover significant feeding damage on vegetables but no slime trail, I suspect cutworms. Common moth species that I find in my garden every year include black cutworm *(Agrotis ipsilon)*, large yellow underwing *(Noctua pronuba)*, and variegated cutworm *(Peridroma saucia)*.

Adult moths in this group are rarely seen because they are nocturnal and lay their eggs on host plants at night. Cutworm larvae are mostly hairless, thickset caterpillars and are often dark brown with white striping. They curl up into a tight "C" when disturbed or when

European cabbage white butterfly *(Pieris rapae)* adult.

resting during the day. Any plant in the garden is a potential meal for a cutworm, but you will find them most easily on large leafy vegetables such as lettuce and cabbage, where they often leave piles of brown excrement in their wake as they feed at night. Frustratingly for the gardener trying to control them, cutworms usually leave the host plant during the day and burrow into the ground.

If you are not interested in searching rows of vegetables at midnight with a flashlight (very effective!) then try this method: using your fingers as a rake, circle around the damaged plant one to two inches down into

the soil. You will find the cutworm within three or four inches of the base of the plant. On large lettuce or cabbage plants, look under any leaves that touch the ground--this is a favorite hiding place for cutworms (and slugs, discussed below). If you keep a close eye on your vegetables, then hand-picking cutworms is very effective. There are many other moth larvae that feed on garden plants but most are transient or cause little damage.

One of the most easily observed garden pests is the European cabbage white butterfly *(Pieris rapae)*. Even if you don't have a vegetable garden, you have likely seen the

This cabbage plant has been damaged by cabbage aphids *(Brevicoryne brassicae)* that stunt its growth.

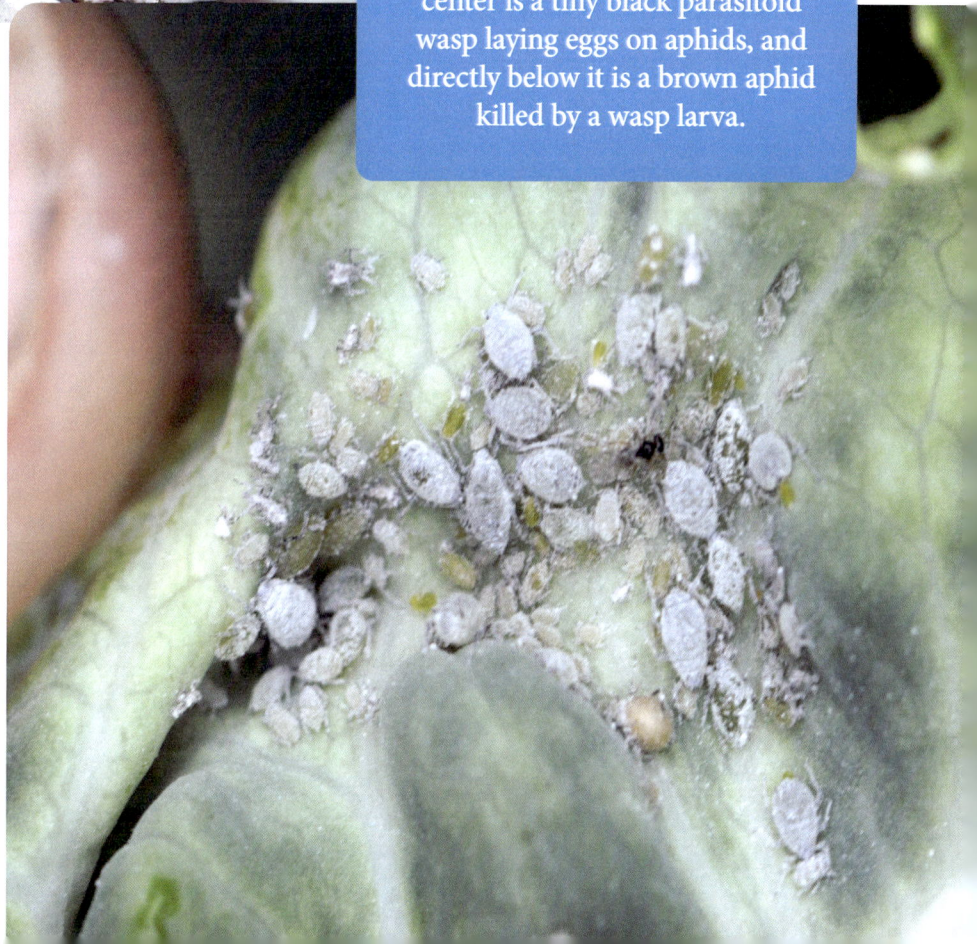

Wingless stage of cabbage aphids, trying to hide in a fold of a distorted cabbage leaf. Near the center is a tiny black parasitoid wasp laying eggs on aphids, and directly below it is a brown aphid killed by a wasp larva.

adults nectaring at flowers. They have white to pale yellow wings with black tips on the forewings; the male has one black spot on his forewing and the female has two black spots on hers. The caterpillar can be very destructive in a garden. It is green and covered with short fine hairs, making it well-camouflaged when it is eating the leaves of its host plants: cabbage, kale, broccoli, turnips, and other members of the mustard family (Brassicaceae). Look for chewed leaves and green

European cabbage white butterfly larvae, well-camouflaged.

piles of moist or watery excrement. Hand picking is adequate to keep the caterpillars from doing significant damage.

You may already have helpers controlling cutworms. My vegetable garden and fruit trees are constantly patrolled by social wasps, particularly yellow jackets and European paper wasps, hunting leaf-eating larvae. They search meticulously, looking in every nook and cranny for a meal. Their nonstop surveillance and removal of pest insects cannot be overrated.

Aphids

Aphids are an abundant and destructive insect. Small and soft-bodied, they suck sap from plants. In a vegetable garden their activity can be quite frustrating because of their ability to reproduce very rapidly. In the process of feeding, some aphids inject toxins into the plants. These toxins cause new growth to become misshapen and leaves and stems to curl. The distorted leaves provide a haven where the aphids can safely feed and

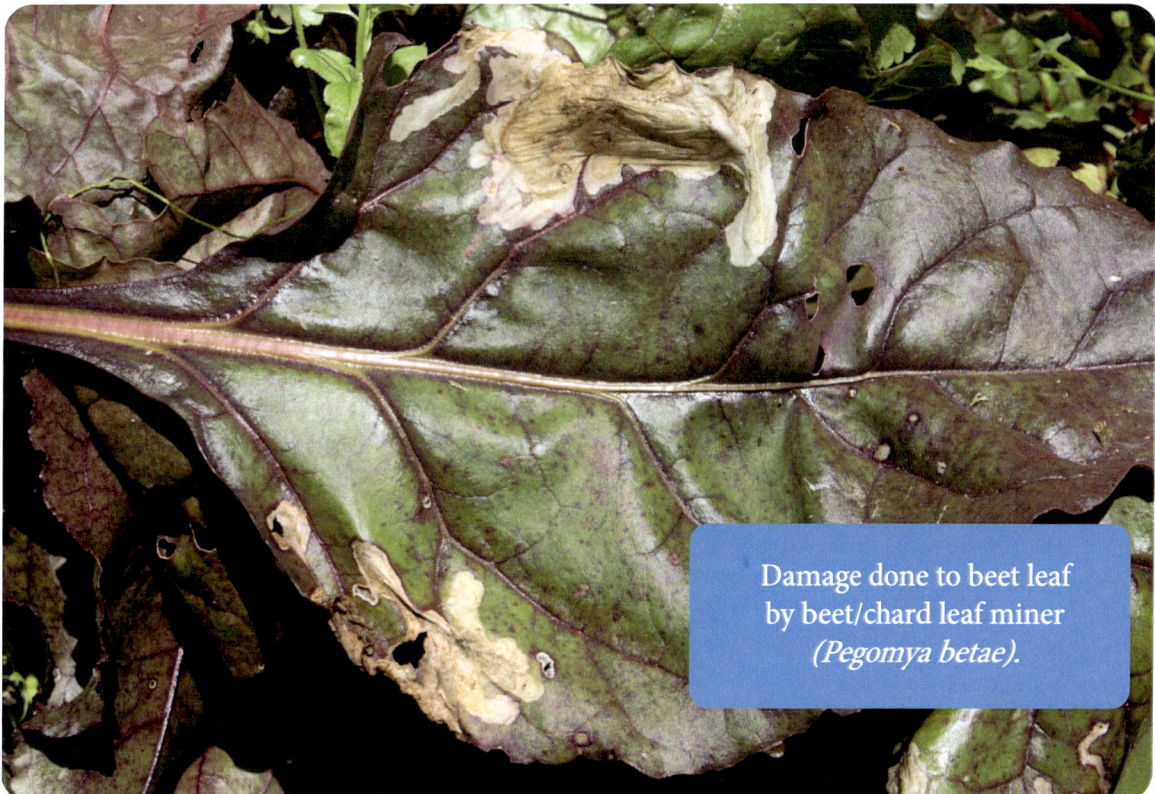

Damage done to beet leaf by beet/chard leaf miner (*Pegomya betae*).

reproduce. Aphids can expel large quantities of a sticky exudate known as honeydew, which builds up on the lower leaves of the plant and often turns black due to the growth of a sooty mold fungus.

Cabbage aphids *(Brevicoryne brassicae)* are especially difficult to control because of their remarkably high fecundity, multiple generations per year, and ability to produce and employ defensive toxins for protection against predators and parasitoids. If you allow pest aphids to survive in early spring, they will be a problem all summer, so early control is imperative. Controlling aphids means constant vigilance and prompt attention! What works? Consistently washing them off plants with a strong stream of water, and crushing small family groups that are found mostly on the underside of leaves. When aphids infest broccoli heads they are especially hard to eradicate, so if necessary I also employ insecticidal soap. It can be very useful if applied directly to the aphids, and it has no systemic or residual toxicity so it won't linger and kill other insects that may be beneficial. Aphids have many predators, but those predators are difficult to attract to

vegetable gardens in sufficient numbers to offer any real population control.

Flies

Most flies are not garden pests, but there are

tissue. The cabbage root maggot *(Delia radicum)* is even harder to control because it stays underground, feeding on the roots of cole plants.

After almost fifty years battling leaf miners and root maggots, I finally tried an insect-blocking row cover. The row covers are almost one hundred percent effective for both types of fly larvae, and as a bonus they work for most other insect pests. I have used the row covers for the last five years, and I find them to be sturdy, reusable, and easy to water through. The only downside is that you have to remove the row covers to weed, but once the vegetable plants become well-established you can take the covers off (although I keep them on as long as possible). In late fall, wash and store the row covers for the winter.

OTHER ARTHROPODS

Sowbugs and pillbugs break down organic material into simpler compounds. They are also a food source for insects, shrews, and birds. While many people consider sowbugs and pillbugs to be pests, they are generally more of a nuisance since they much prefer

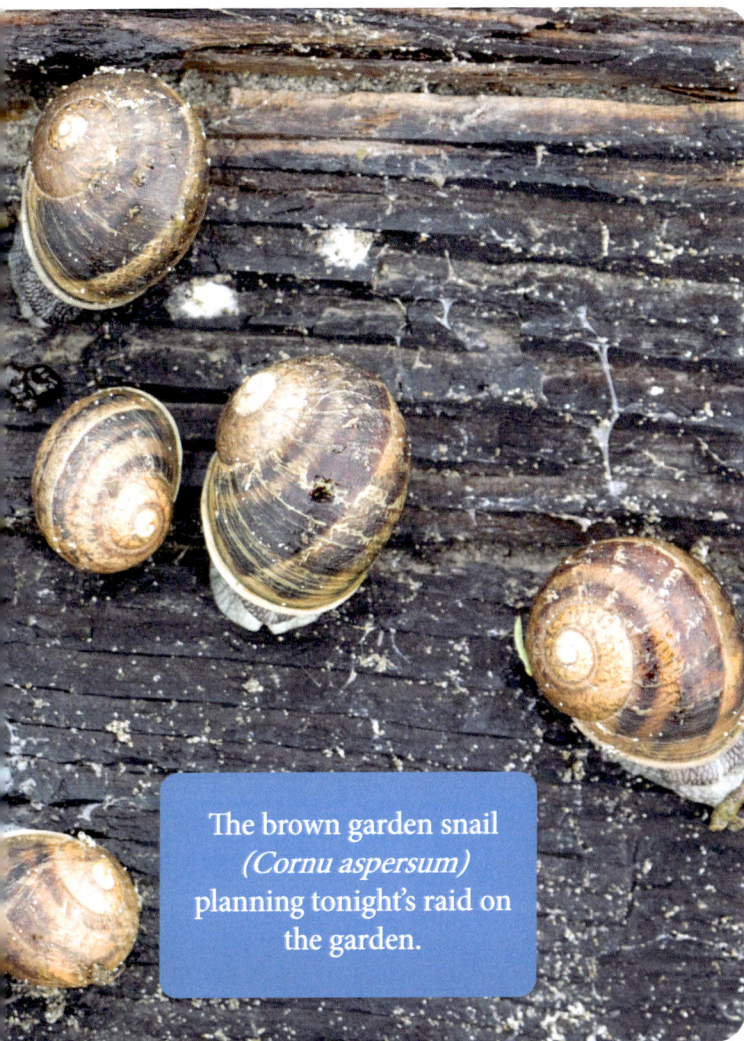

The brown garden snail *(Cornu aspersum)* planning tonight's raid on the garden.

two fly species whose larvae long evaded my efforts to control them on vegetables. The beet/chard leaf miner *(Pegomya betae)* is unaffected by most predators and insecticides because it lives between layers of the host plant's

Chocolate arion (*Arion ater* complex) "dark form."

decaying vegetation to live plants. If you do find sowbugs or pillbugs to be a problem, try keeping the area around the base of each plant free of dead or dying leaves to discourage them. Neither of these "bugs" are insects—they are crustaceans, and are more closely related to crabs and shrimp than to insects. To determine if you've found a pillbug or a sowbug, check for two small tail-like appendages. Sowbugs have them; pillbugs don't. Also, pillbugs can roll into a tight ball, while sowbugs can't.

Molluscs

For many gardeners, the most despised pests in the garden are snails and slugs. Though we deploy pesticides, beer traps, copper barriers, the soles of our shoes, and more, they seem to come in endless waves, plundering our gardens no matter what we do. Be sure to identify slugs and snails carefully, since there are predaceous snail species that are garden helpers rather than garden competitors (See Chapter 3 for more information).

Snails

The brown garden snail *(Cornu aspersum)* was introduced to California from Europe in the 1850s for use as escargot. Subsequently, Americans lost interest in dining on snails, but the brown garden snail has long since spread throughout the Pacific Northwest and now lives in our gardens and dines on our plants. The snail's shell is yellow-brown with irregular markings and streaks, creating a banded appearance, and its body is grey to pale brown. While the brown garden snail will eat a wide range of plants, its favorite is young succulent plant tissues. If you discover heavily damaged new growth on your plants, look for dried slime—a telltale sign of the culprit. The brown garden snail is a night feeder, but warm spring and fall showers or summer irrigation can bring it out during the day. Though snails are slow-moving, they can travel long distances at night and then seek shelter before dawn.

Slugs

Another slimy culprit, comparable in size to an adult banana slug, is the non-native chocolate arion slug (Arion ater complex), of which there are several color variations, though all have heavily wrin-

Slug eggs: the chocolate arion lays its eggs on the soil surface, while the brown garden snail lays its eggs underground.

kled skin and a striped reddish foot fringe. Its size and appetite for tender young vegetables makes it the most problematic slug in many gardens, and it requires constant vigilance year-round.

Chocolate arion (*Arion ater* complex) "light form."

The gray garden slug *(Deroceras reticulatum)*, a synanthropic (thriving in habitats that are disturbed by humans) native of Europe, is now found worldwide. It is medium to small in size, and variable in color though commonly gray or brown with a reticulate pattern of black spots or lines. When threatened it produces a milky mucus for protection. The gray garden slug considers any plant in the garden a potential meal, but like all slugs it is most destructive to tender young plants.

An easy first step to both controlling slugs and attracting their predators is to place untreated wooden boards between vegetable rows or near groups of plants that you want to protect. The soil under these planks provides a dark, damp environment where slugs, snails, and cutworms will hide during the day. Once every three to five days, simply

The gray garden slug *(Deroceras reticulatum).*

turn over the boards and crush the slugs and snails you find there, including their pearly white egg masses. This method of control is easy, nontoxic, and safe, and it allows you to monitor pest populations on a regular basis. After some time you will notice that the slugs that cause the most damage—large adults—become uncommon.

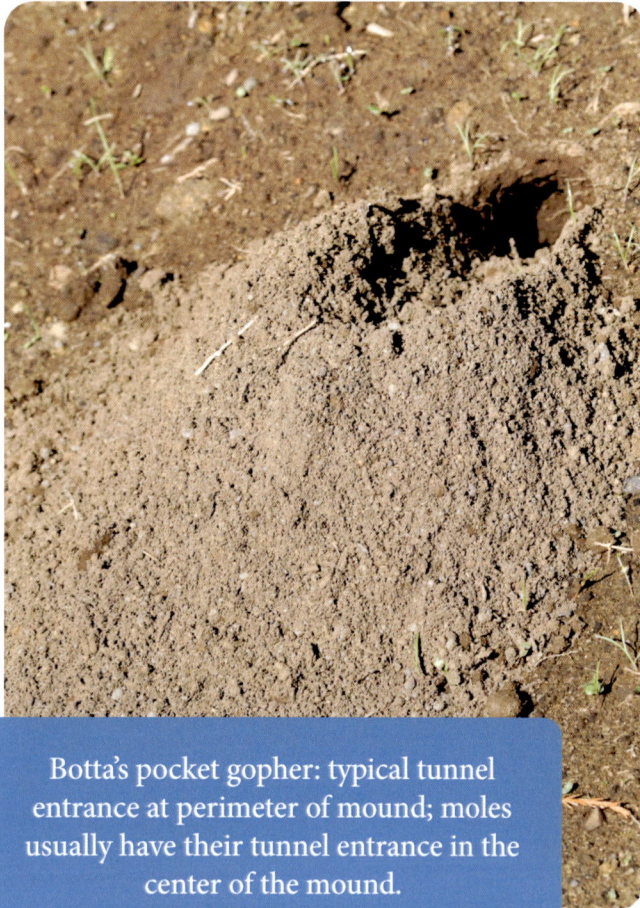

Botta's pocket gopher: typical tunnel entrance at perimeter of mound; moles usually have their tunnel entrance in the center of the mound.

What's more, these same wooden boards create a safe place where helpful predators—especially beetles--can also hide during the day. In Chapter 3 I described several of these species. All of them are predators as adult and larva, and will consume slugs, snails, and cutworms. In moderate climates they can be active much of the year. Many of these predators are flightless and must live and reproduce close to their food supply—that is, directly in the garden or very close to it.

MAMMALS

Living with other mammals in a wildlife garden can be like living with human *(Homo sapiens)* neighbors: complex and sometimes frustrating. Some mammals you may never notice as they go about their busy lives, like voles (genus *Microtus*), shrews *(Sorex vagrans)*, and gray foxes *(Urocyon cinereoargenteus)*. Others, such as Botta's pocket gopher *(Thomomys bottae)*, can be a constant threat to vegetable gardens and newly planted fruit trees, especially stone fruits. But there are many ways we can remain on reasonably good terms with most wildlife, including mammals.

Botta's pocket gopher *(Thomomys bottae)* adult clearing dirt from its tunnel entrance.

Botta's pocket gopher is a stocky rodent with very large front teeth and big cheek pouches. Altogether a very handsome rodent! But my assessment of Botta's pocket gopher turns negative when I see my garlic plants whipping back and forth and find that the garlic bulb has been consumed. To be fair, when not eating garden plants the gophers dig tunnels, which aerate the soil, improve water drainage, and provide homes for snakes, lizards, and bumble bee colonies.

To protect your vegetables from gophers, raised beds with hardware cloth underneath work well. Wire baskets, sold at garden nurseries, can protect newly planted fruit trees. Trapping, while not for everyone, can be very effective. When I see a fresh gopher mound within seven to ten feet of my vegetable garden or orchard, I start trapping.

Many other potential mammal problems can be avoided by maintaining a "clean" garden. Eliminate unsecured garbage and mulch, never leave pet foods outside, and don't let your bird feeders become messy. By having a "messy" garden, we teach animals like rats, raccoons, skunks, and bears that they can find easy meals around human habitation, and they then become very troublesome. However, if they can't get an easy meal in your garden, they will move along.

While I see skunks and raccoons in my yard on a nightly basis, they seldom cause trouble. Raccoons, like bears, cannot be excluded from a garden without the use of

Mule deer *(Odocoileus hemionus)* eating "my" apples (the deer is on the outside of our deer-proof fence).

electrified fencing, so keep your garden and yard tidy and free of potential food. Be aware that many animals are protected by state and provincial regulations throughout the Pacific Northwest.

Keeping the garden clean also means you will have fewer issues with rodents (including rats). Squirrels, other small rodents, and rabbits have never been a problem for me because our neighborhood has so many free ranging cats! If small rodents and rabbits are a serious issue for you, use insect fabric on your vegetable rows. While meant to keep insects out, it also helps prevent rodent depredation.

Then there are deer. The mule deer (*Odocoileus hemionus*) is the last large herbivore still living in the Pacific Northwest where urban conditions allow. It has adapted well to "city life" but definitely also needs natural areas for feeding, raising young, and resting. Deer roam my neighborhood on a daily basis and they would be sorely missed if lost from our community.

Deer can be devastating to a young orchard and to ornamental plants, eating the buds and branches in the spring and, in the case of male deer, scraping the velvet off their antlers in the fall. The only permanent solution to a

> **Having a wildlife garden means sharing a space with native wildlife**

deer problem is a deer-proof fence. Since I installed fencing thirty years ago I have had zero problems with deer. If you have a small yard where wire deer-proof fencing and posts would be impractical, many farm and feed stores sell lightweight plastic fencing that is easy to install when needed (and to remove when not needed). One option is to place the fence around your garden plot or orchard rather than your whole yard. While I have not used portable electric fencing, I believe it would work as well as regular deer-proof fencing while being much easier to set up.

Having a wildlife garden means sharing a space with native wildlife. Being able to both protect your garden plants and share the garden with wild mammals is definitely a balancing act, but well worth the effort.

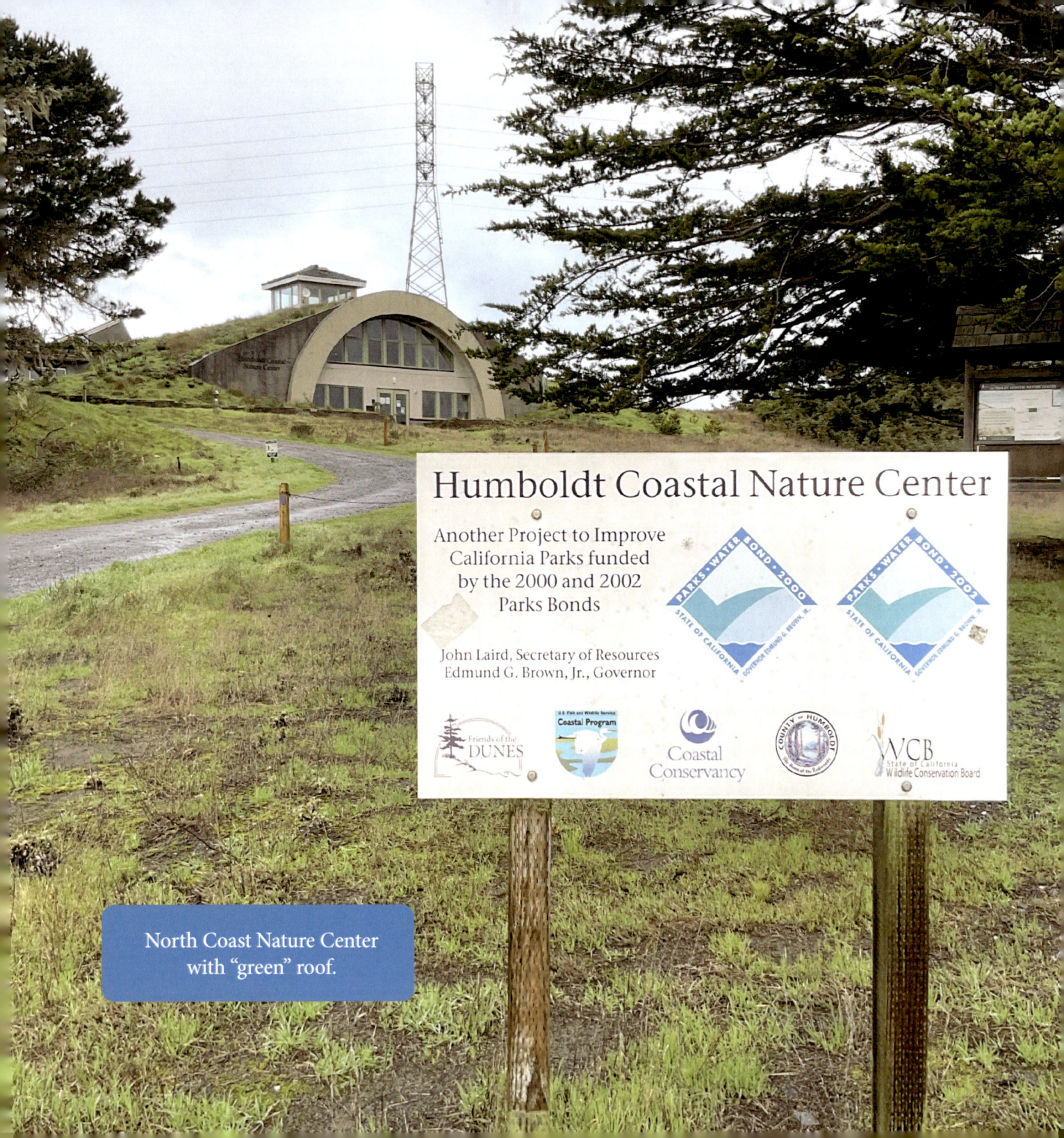

Humboldt Coastal Nature Center

Another Project to Improve
California Parks funded
by the 2000 and 2002
Parks Bonds

John Laird, Secretary of Resources
Edmund G. Brown, Jr., Governor

North Coast Nature Center
with "green" roof.

GARDEN MAINTENANCE: A STABLE LANDSCAPE

6

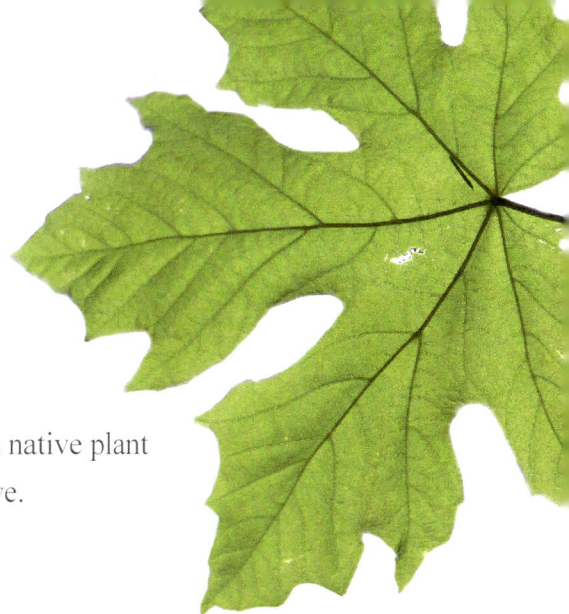

I have helped plan and maintain five public native plant/wildlife gardens in the Humboldt Bay area. While this may or may not make me an expert, I have learned a lot through experience, and I still maintain two of these gardens. The Arcata Community Center Native Plant and Wildlife Garden was planted in 1999 and boasts native trees, shrubs, herbaceous perennials, and annuals. It provides waves of flowers from spring through late fall for native pollinators and the people of Arcata. The second garden is a sand dune plant community on the roof of the Friends of the Dunes North Coast Nature Center, planted in 2011. The priority here is to stabilize the sand on the roof and perimeter of the Nature Center while still maintaining the original diversity of the dune mat community. Both gardens have their own unique requirements and both have helped me be a better gardener. Though their plant communities have different needs, there are several basic features that require attention to make sure that they—and your own native plant garden—thrive.

Irrigation

A good rule for irrigation is to use the minimal amount of water that will keep the plants alive and healthy. But, like all rules, it needs to be broken now and then. For a new planting, extra water is necessary to help the plants get established.

The first three years after starting your native plant garden are critical for ensuring that woody plants and herbaceous perennials are going to succeed long term. The further you are from the coast, the more important irrigation can be, especially in low elevation inland valleys that have hot dry summers. It's best to plant the woody perennials first so that they can start to modify the garden's microclimate via the shade, wind protection, and soil stabilization that woody plants provide. The root zone should be mulched to protect against

Arcata Community Center Native Plant and Wildlife Garden.

extreme changes in moisture level and soil temperature (to prevent disease. keep the mulch away from the base of the plant). Eventually the plant roots will reach deeper soil and increases in leaf litter will provide protection. Inland valleys or extremely windy sites need wind and shade protection. You can purchase tree shelters through forestry and nursery catalogs and websites or, even better, make your own custom shelter using plant stakes and shade fabric.

All of my new plantings are hand watered but I live close to the coast where the summers are mild. I enjoy hand watering, but if it isn't an option for you, I recommend drip irrigation. Done correctly, drip irrigation makes watering much easier, though a poor setup can be water wasteful or get plugged up, so make sure your system is installed correctly from the start. Overhead broadcast watering, as with a sprinkler system, is a very poor choice for several reasons: It wastes water, increases leaf

There are at least four genera of powdery mildew that affect oaks. Oregon white oak *(Quercus garryana)* and other oaks are susceptible to powdery mildew infections from overhead watering.

diseases by encouraging fungal growth, and stimulates weed seed germination so that you will have much more weeding to do. Overly lush growth from too much water will produce leaves and stems that are soft and susceptible to diseases and pests.

To make the job of watering easier, try to group plants according to their water needs. For instance, willows, twinberry, and checkerbloom appreciate summer water and often produce more flowers and seeds when irrigated. However, oaks, manzanita, and buckwheat prefer little or no summer water and in fact can get leaf diseases and root rot if watered during the summer.

Twenty-four-inch tall shore pine *(Pinus contorta)* pruned for a small native plant garden.

Fertilizing

No matter the soil type, I don't use fertilizer on my plants, with few exceptions. I do use foliar applications of fertilizer on cole crops and corn in the vegetable garden. Fertilization of native plants can cause fast growth, but slow and steady plant growth is preferable, because it results in a better balance of leaves to roots—and an overall

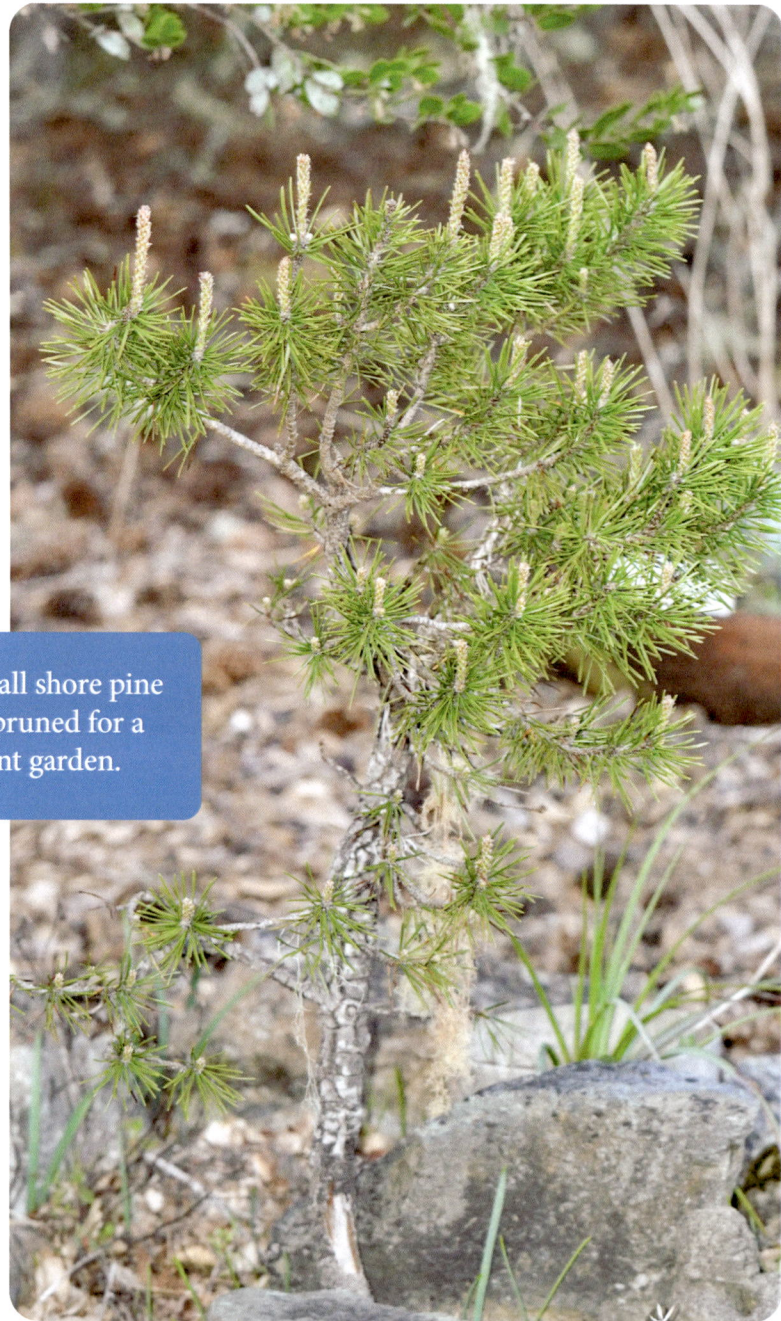

healthier, stronger plant. New, fast-growing leaves are not as sturdy or disease-resistant as "toughened" leaves. The sooner that new leaves toughen up, the better they can withstand heat, lack of water, and pathogens, and the less palatable they are to leaf eaters.

Fertilizers encourage weeds, which are a constant problem in a developing garden.

Many annual weeds and perennial weedy grasses are shallow-rooted, so their roots can reach and absorb fertilizer and water before the deeper-rooted plants. When plant nutrients are at their natural levels, plants are better able to compete with invasive weeds. Adding fertilizer to the garden changes this delicate balance in favor of the weeds by speeding up their growth.

Taller shore pine left unpruned for a larger garden.

Besides making life harder for your plants, fertilizers are also hard on the environment. High nitrogen fertilizers in particular are overused in urban gardens, parks, golf courses, and agriculture, and their production and overuse cause environmental problems. Excess nitrogen that enters waterways and lakes causes "blooms" of algae and other water weeds that can cover the water surface, reduce oxygen in the water, cause fish die offs, and replace native vegetation.

Pruning

Early on while the plants are establishing themselves is the best time to decide if you want to keep your woody plants pruned or let them grow naturally. Plant pruning is an art; you do not need to follow a particular pruning system, but learn the proper pruning techniques to keep your plants healthy. To avoid introducing pathogens, prune during dry periods, keep your tools sharp and clean, and learn how to determine which limbs

Maintained piles of wood or tree bark provide excellent wildlife habitat summer and winter.

Silktassel *(Garrya elliptica)* pruned to about ten feet tall, with base opened up to allow shade tolerant plants to grow underneath.

may be weak or diseased. Heavy pruning is normally done during the dormant season (usually winter), but light pruning can be done year-round.

In a small garden it is often best to employ regular pruning to maintain a balance of trees, shrubs, and annual and perennial herbaceous plants. I use pruning to keep trees like beach pine and tall shrubs like silktassel (genus *Garrya*) under ten feet tall and give them a more open, mature look. Open pruning allows more sunlight and air to reach the interior limbs. The increased sun and airflow make the leaves and branches less susceptible to disease.

Personality and Safe Havens

Early in the life of your native garden is the perfect time to add wildlife shelters and homes such as logs, piles of rocks or branches, small water features, bird houses, or art. All of these will not only provide safe havens for wildlife, but will also give your garden even more personality.

Logs should be partially buried in the soil so that they will retain moisture during the summer. A well placed log provides a suitably damp shelter for toads, frogs, salamanders, and many invertebrates, especially predaceous ground beetles and centipedes.

Rock and brush piles are used by lizards, toads, and snakes to escape heat and predators and to reproduce in. Piles of brush or branches provide safety and nesting sites for small mammals. Brush piles will need to be replenished yearly—use garden prunings. Arrange rocks so there are plenty of small crawl spaces for wildlife to enter and exit.

A small water feature in your garden will serve multiple purposes: breeding sites for amphibians, drinking water for various animals, and a home for aquatic insects like dragonflies. Stock tanks (sold at feed stores) made of durable plastic work quite well as small ponds. Even a container as small as five gallons can provide breeding habitat for Pacific tree frogs and dragonflies. Containers with steep sides will discourage mosquitos from breeding. In late summer and fall, water features become very important sources of drinking water for birds and will need to be replenished frequently with clean, fresh water.

Because bird species such as chickadees and bluebirds often have a hard time finding housing, adding sturdy nest boxes to your garden can be very helpful. When deciding where to place a nest

Tree bark covered with leaves or compost provides damp year-round hideaways for frogs, salamanders, and invertebrates.

Various predaceous beetle species are often found under piles of wood, bark or tree branches.

box, keep in mind that birds prefer vegetation near their nesting site. Why? For safety reasons: They can land in the vegetation and evaluate the area around the nest before flying into it. If you have fruit trees, place the nest boxes near them so that adults with hungry nestlings make their first insect-foraging stop in your orchard.

We humans are part of any wildlife garden, as architects, designers, and most importantly as maintenance stewards.

I think that the inclusion of art or homemade crafts can be done in a non-intrusive way. Perhaps a monolith--a large, single upright block of stone--can

Many insect species benefit from dead trees, including leafcutter bees (genus *Megachile*) and mason bees (genus *Osmia*), which often nest in deadwood: these pupal bee cells made of leaves are in chambers hollowed out in deadwood.

Douglas-fir needles and cones left on the ground provide deer mice (genus *Peromyscus*) with plenty of food and nesting material.

Wildlife pond at summer's end. This pond provides habitat for frog and toad tadpoles, salamander larvae, overwintering insects, and three-spined stickleback fish.

years by high shade as the majority of lower branches are shade-pruned. With these transformations come changes in suitability of different parts of the garden for different plant species.

Dense shade is best for deep-forest plants like ferns, wild ginger, and trilliums, while yerba buena, vanilla grass, and many species of violets prefer high shade. Plants like strawberry, columbine, mock orange, and Ithuriel's spear appreciate full sun or partial shade. In hot inland valleys, the presence of shady areas can mean survival for some plants and animals. Snakes, lizards, birds, and many insects need a shady green oasis during the day.

New niches also develop below ground as the soil in the garden becomes better aerated by plant roots and tunneling

represent our long-term personal commitment to the garden. Keep your garden denizens in mind, but be creative!

New niches

As your landscape grows and becomes more biodiverse new niches will appear, most obviously as regards shade and sun. In five to ten years, dense shade will develop under trees and large shrubs, followed in a few

animals. Organic material builds up both above and below ground as leaves fall and roots die, which makes the soil much more hospitable for fungi (including mushrooms) and for invertebrates like worms, millipedes, and insects. The duff layer that slowly builds on the soil surface is a new refuge for animals seeking shelter from a hot dry summer and invertebrates overwintering under plants. Every new niche adds to the complexity of the garden and its long-term stability.

Patches of bare ground are a very important niche, used by nesting native bees and seed-eating birds when scratching for food. Many birds also love taking dust baths in these bare areas. Irregularly spaced bare spots will also make a landscape more natural-looking.

Tidying Up

Keeping a wildlife garden neat and tidy is not a requirement but can be beneficial. About once every one to three years, I run a

Two recently emerged adult dragonflies (the cardinal meadowhawk, *Sympetrum illotum*) that spent their nymphal stages in a small pond.

Areas with moist soil and dense shade are the perfect habitat for perennial plants like this stream violet *(Viola glabella).*

lawn mower over semi-woody herbaceous perennials that have become leggy, such as *Phacelia*, gumweed (genus *Grindelia*), and asters (genus *Symphyotrichum*). Removing their aging stems stimulates new growth and results in more flowers in the summer. In areas where wildfires occur, removal of fire hazards around buildings is essential.

Fruit and Vegetables

In some ways, growing vegetables is the opposite of a native plant garden. We remove the vegetation, plant vegetables that have long been cultivated by humans, pull weeds, water, and provide fertilizer if needed. Vegetable gardening teaches us what it takes to grow food and tend the soil while dealing directly with nature in the form of rain, drought, bugs, slugs, and more. Growing your own food makes you more sophisticated about life, not just gardening!

I use as little fertilizer or organic material from off site as possible. That means the vegetables get minimal fertilizing, and when they do need enrichment, I only use kitchen compost or foliar fertilizers. Soil fertility is maintained with green manure. In hot inland

Crimson clover *(Trifolium incarnatum)* makes an excellent green manure for maintaining vegetable garden productivity. On the left, crimson clover densely planted and in full flower; on the right, the crimson clover was allowed to go to seed and then plowed under.

areas where soil dries out rapidly, compost may be necessary around vegetables to maintain consistent moisture levels. After one year of vegetables on a plot, that site gets one to two years of green manure (my preference is crimson clover) to enrich the soil. This cycle also helps reduce soil related diseases and pests such as root rot (including *Phytophthora*), vascular wilts caused by fungi (including *Verticillium*), nematodes, and insect pests like root maggots.

I have tried to evaluate my garden and production of vegetables objectively over the last nine years, and while the routine I outlined above works great, the total weight of cole and leaf crops is less than if I was using commercial or organic fertilizers from off site (though most vegetables show no difference). Large infusions of high-nitrogen fertilizers (whether organic or chemical) are simply not necessary to maintain sufficient soil fertility for a healthy vegetable garden. The production and use of commercial fertilizers carries huge environmental costs. I decided many years ago that the slight drop in cole and leaf crop harvest was quite acceptable.

While I try to use the minimum amount of water in my spring and summer vegetable garden, I still end up watering regularly. Our Pacific Northwest summers are usually dry, and water is essential for healthy produce, especially seedlings, cole crops, and lettuce.

Weeding

Many of the most pesky weeds

When cleaning up the garden in winter remember to leave some upright woody stems so that solitary bees like this mason bee have a place to build nests.

in the vegetable garden
are synanthropic, meaning
they benefit from living
alongside humans, and most
are of Eurasian origin, having
accompanied European colonists
to North America. Sheep sorrel
(Rumex acetosella), annual
bluegrass *(Poa annua)*, crabgrass
(genus *Digitaria*), and others
require human manipulation of a
landscape: cultivation, planting,
watering, and weeding to help
them thrive. Over thousands of
years of weeding we humans
have inadvertently selected
for the very hardiest plants to
compete with our vegetables.

In the vegetable garden there
are no easy answers for weeding.
I have only one garden tool for
weeds (other than my hands):
the diamond headed hoe. This
hoe makes weeding much easier
because it is able to cut weeds
below the surface whether moving
forward or backward. Because it

Fall bounty from an espaliered tree: comice pear.

has pointed ends you can be very precise in weeding around tender young plants.

The Orchard, or Just a Fruit Tree or Two

Apple and pear trees are very much at home in the Pacific Northwest. They are tolerant of wet feet in the winter, which can mean death for stone fruits. All of my fruit trees are on dwarf rootstock, which gives them a mature height of eight to twelve feet and makes orchard maintenance such as pruning, pest and disease control, and harvesting much easier. Not having to use a ladder when pruning and harvesting is also safer.

Another benefit of dwarf fruit trees: They allow you to fit more varieties in the same space as one standard fruit tree. I train or prune my apples and pears to a modified espalier with one to three horizontal branches. This allows more air movement and sunlight to penetrate the interior of the tree, which in turn means fewer diseases like apple scab *(Venturia inaequalis)* and pear scab *(Venturia pirina)*. In hot interior valleys, this open tree

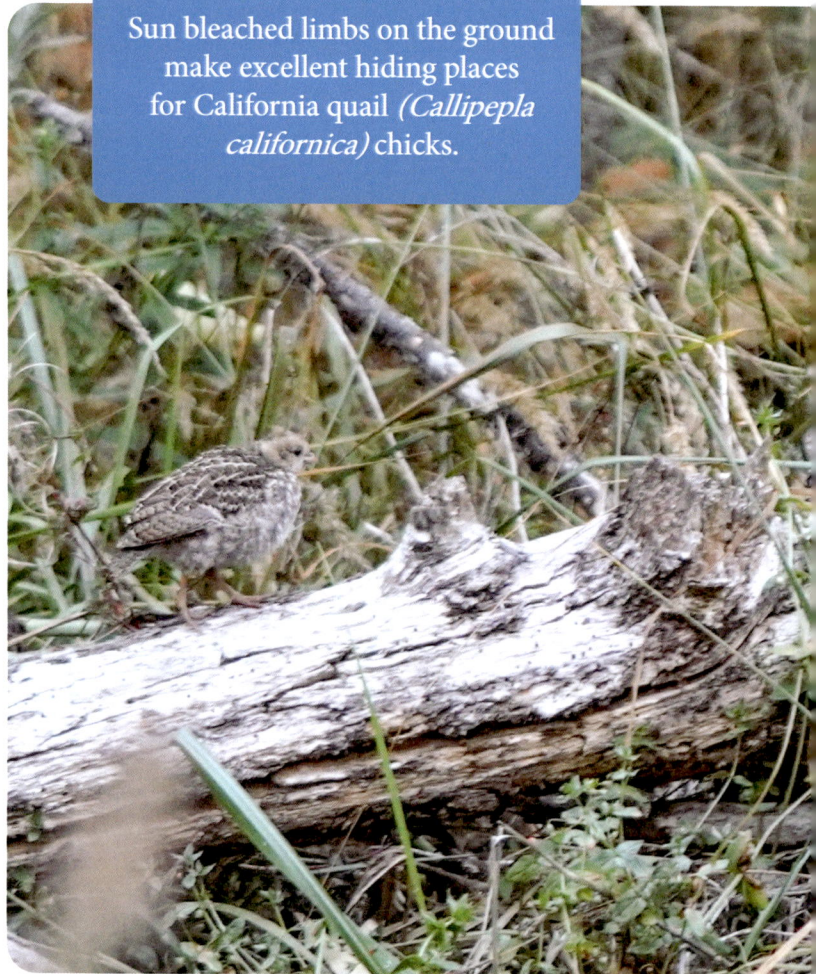

Sun bleached limbs on the ground make excellent hiding places for California quail *(Callipepla californica)* chicks.

structure may have to be modified because it could cause sunscald on trees and fruit.

Fruit tree diseases such as scab, mildew, and fireblight should be treated prophylactically. Once you see an infection on the leaves or fruit, it is too late to apply

protection. In late winter I apply a trunk barrier such as Tanglefoot to the bases of all my fruit trees. This prevents ants from climbing into the trees where they will defend the aphids that are feeding on the fruit trees. Without the ants' protection, natural predators like ladybird beetles and soldier beetles are able to control aphids.

Winter Break

Winter is a good time to evaluate whether the wildlife refuge woodpiles need replenishing, the bare soil for nesting bees needs to be maintained, or bird nest boxes need repairs or cleaning before spring.

If you use a water feature to encourage frogs and insects such as dragonflies or damselflies to breed, make sure it includes native water plants for tadpoles and insects to hide among. Purchase a small net from a pet store and use it to check for the immature stages of insects overwintering in your pond. In late winter, look for masses of frog eggs or tadpoles among the water plants. Raccoons are a constant threat to any water feature, especially if it contains frogs or tadpoles. A very effective way to discourage raccoons from raiding the pond is to use coarse netting. Cut it to the shape of the pond but large enough to overlap the edges, and simply lay it on top. The bird netting allows tree frogs easy access to the water but discourages raccoons from "fishing" for the frogs.

Winter is best for analyzing the garden landscape as a whole because you can easily see its underlying structure. Deciduous plants are leafless, annuals are gone, and the backbone of the landscape is clearly visible. Even though I try to work in the garden as often as possible, sometimes it's necessary to step back and look at it with fresh eyes. Appreciate it not as a place where you work but as a home for native plants, wildlife, and you, twenty-four hours a day, and give yourself a generous pat on the back, job well done!

Isabella tiger moth (aka banded woolly bear) *(Pyrrharctia isabella)* caterpillars, overwintering in tree hole.

NATURAL HISTORY 7

The underlying theme of every chapter in this book: No matter where you live, make your home and garden an intrinsic part of nature. In this chapter I will describe the colorful natural histories of a few of the animals I have had in my garden. I hope this will encourage you to provide a space for them and learn more about the extraordinary animals that share your world.

The Story of Spike

Every spring I walk along the banks of a local river where sand and gravel are commercially mined. I carry a small fish net and a one-gallon jug with the top half cut off. The heavy equipment used to mine the gravel leaves shallow ponds that attract western toads *(Anaxyrus boreas)*, who lay eggs in communal masses that fill the ponds. The mining ponds dry up long before all of the tadpoles can mature into toads. When I see that the ponds are drying up and

Western toad *(Anaxyrus boreas)* tadpoles in shallow pool.

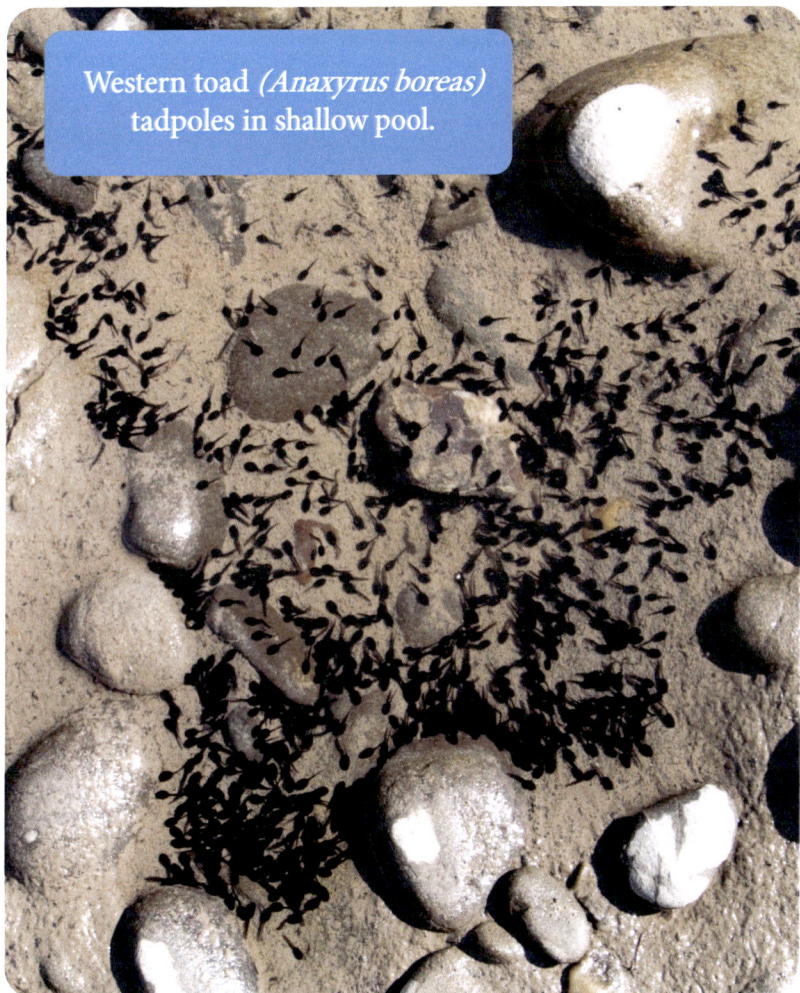

Spike the toad living in gopher hole in vegetable garden.

the tadpoles have no hope of surviving. I start transferring hundreds of them from the ponds to the river or to larger ponds that are closer to the river. I also take a few tadpoles home with me and put them in the small pond in my yard.

This is how I first met Spike. Could I possibly recognize this tiny pollywog from among the thousands of his brethren (and sistren)? Of course I could: Spike was the cutest one! I brought him home where he matured into a toadlet and left our small pond in midsummer. In late spring of the following year he was living in a gopher hole with two other toads in our vegetable garden. By fall of that year he left his roommates and excavated a hole under a flat stone closer to our house and to the pond where he grew up.

Both my wife, Judy, and I love toads and by the following spring we had started making

Spike digging underground shelter using back feet.

friends with Spike. Toads are mostly nocturnal but apparently, like people, hungry both day and night. I communicated with Spike by tapping on the stone roof of his home during the day. When he sensed the tapping, his eyes opened, and I wiggled a worm, slug, or cricket in front of him. At first he would cautiously eye the bait before very slowly emerging from his lair. When he saw the bait move, he shot out his tongue and swallowed his prey. If the tidbit was a slug, it would usually leave slimy mud or other debris on his lips, which he would wipe clean with his front legs. His table manners were always impeccable and his face always clean.

Through that year and the next, Judy and I formed an interspecies bond with Spike. At night he hunted in our garden and by day we entertained our neighbors by tapping on the roof of his home and watching as he waddled out to be hand fed. But our friendship came to an abrupt end in the winter of Spike's third year. The instinct to reproduce drove him to leave our garden in pursuit of a mate and water to breed. It was a lonely spring and summer for Judy and I, but hopefully not for Spike. Every spring since Spike left, I wander the mining pools along the river looking for Spike, Jr. Will I see hints of him in his tadpole offspring, I wonder?

Spike enjoying a savory slug.

Woolly Bears, Woolly Worms

Why do some animals sport bright colors or eye-catching patterns? And is there an answer to the age-old question, "Why do woolly bears cross the road?"? Woolly bear caterpillars become nice and plump from grazing all summer on tender vegetation. As cold and rainy weather approaches, it is time for them to find a dry, safe place to spend the winter. That is why every year in late fall you see so many woolly bear caterpillars "crossing the road".

The woolly bear or woolly worm (caterpillars of the tiger moth family, Erebidae) is not really woolly but covered with long stiff hairs called setae that give it a cute, fuzzy teddy-bear appearance. When disturbed it often curls into a tight ball to protect its hairless underside. Handling the woolly bear carefully will prevent harm to larva and handler.

There are a few common species of woolly bears or woolly worms that you might find in your garden, none of which are garden pests: the rusty orange and black Isabella tiger moth or banded woolly bear *(Pyrrharctia isabella)* caterpillar, the yellow-spotted tiger moth *(Lophocampa maculata)* caterpillar, the yellow Virginia tiger moth *(Spilosoma virginica)* caterpillar, and the ranchman's

Yellow-spotted tiger moth *(Lophocampa maculata)* caterpillars, two color variations, fall.

tiger moth *(Arctia virginalis)* caterpillar. Most woolly bears eat herbaceous nonwoody plants such as English plantain, dandelions, grasses, and clovers.

Often the adults and larvae of tiger moths are conspicuously colored or patterned. The caterpillars are usually slow-moving, and the adults reluctant to fly. This seems like the perfect prey for a hungry bird, yet when you see woolly bears crossing streets and sidewalks in large numbers during the fall, you may notice that birds show no interest in them.

Aposematism is the display of bright colors or distinctive patterns to warn predators that the possible prey tastes bad or can be unpleasant to eat. Predators learn, by having a bad dining experience, that these larvae are best avoided. Imagine a young bird seeing a fat juicy woolly bear for the first time, picking it up, and trying to swallow it. When the woolly bear's stiff hairs come in contact with the bird's tender throat it must feel like trying to swallow a porcupine! From then on, that bird will ignore the colorful plump woolly bears when searching for food.

Chemical Protection

Woolly bears use hairs as physical

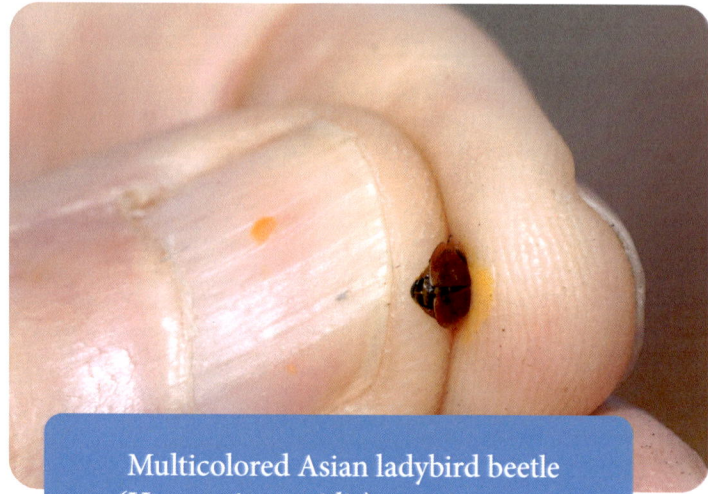

Multicolored Asian ladybird beetle *(Harmonia axyridis)* secreting orange defensive chemical when squeezed.

Ranchman's tiger moth *(Arcia virginalis)* caterpillars, spring.

Virginia tiger moth *(Spilosoma virginica)* caterpillar, late fall. The yellow color seems to glow in foggy weather.

Overwintering convergent ladybird beetles *(Hippodamia convergens)* are protected from predation by aposematic coloring and chemical repellents.

or mechanical deterrents to predation, but many other aposematic invertebrates use chemical deterrents. For example, if a colorfully patterned tiger moth is attacked, it can produce a noxious bubbly ooze of pyrrolizidine alkaloids (a predator repellent) from glands on the dorsal sides of the thorax. One taste provides a memorably bad experience for the predator rather than an easy meal.

As many a curious child knows, when you pick up and examine an adult ladybird beetle you may notice that it exudes a smelly, finger-staining yellowish liquid. An inexperienced predator quickly learns that this chemical repellent is unpalatable. That is how the convergent ladybird beetle *(Hippodamia convergens)* can overwinter in large, highly visible aggregations without significant predation.

Mating pair of yellow-spotted cyanide millipedes *(Harpaphe haydeniana).*

Bird dropping mimic: Western tiger swallowtail (*Papilio rutulus*) first larval instar.

Another invertebrate that relies on chemical compounds to keep itself safe is the yellow-spotted millipede (*Harpaphe haydeniana*), also known as the cyanide millipede, which is common in the wet forests along the Pacific Coast of North America. If disturbed or handled, this flat-backed species oozes hydrogen cyanide and benzaldehyde, which smell of bitter almonds and act as predator repellents. As far as I am aware, the only predators that eat cyanide millipedes are carabid beetles in the genus Promecognathus and a glow worm in the family Phengodidae (genus *Zarhipis*).

The western tiger swallowtail (*Papilio rutulus*) is one of the most common garden butterflies in the coastal Pacific Northwest during the summer. Caterpillars in the family Papilionidae have an eversible gland called an osmeterium that functions as a multipurpose defensive organ. The osmeterium resembles a snake's fleshy forked tongue which, along with the eyespots on the caterpillar's thorax, provides a visual warning to predators. Further, the osmeterium emits defensive chemicals. When the caterpillar is disturbed in any way, the osmeterium is everted and a foul, disagreeable odor is produced that

Later instar caterpillars of the Western tiger swallowtail are green with eyespots.

reduces predation by ants and other invertebrate predators.

Freeloaders

Boring day! How about a trip to the garden for some fang and claw?

One spring when the fruit trees were blooming I saw a crab spider catch a honey bee. Once the bee stopped struggling and the crab spider started feeding, I noticed tiny red-eyed flies arriving and landing near the pair. The flies approached closer and examined the dead bee, then appeared to find a good spot to start feeding. After a long search through my

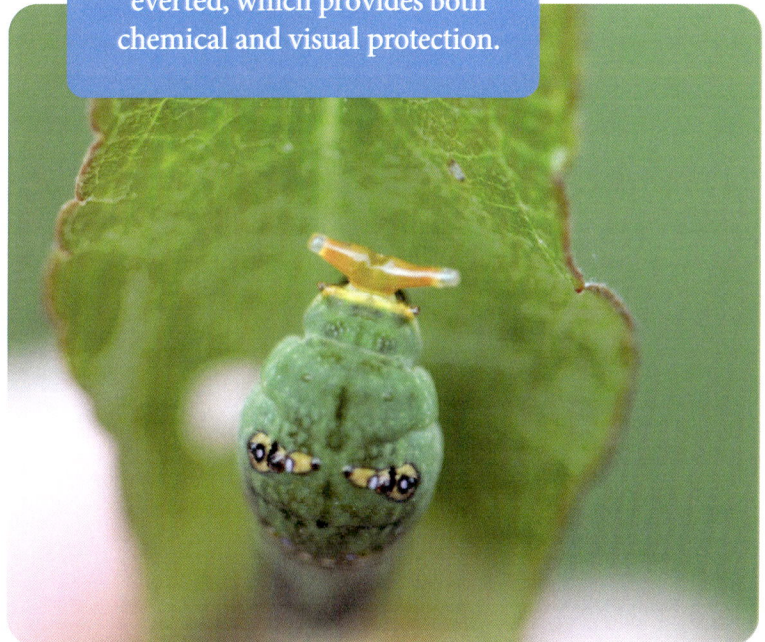

Western tiger swallowtail caterpillar with osmeterium everted, which provides both chemical and visual protection.

Crab spider and freeloader flies feeding on a honey bee.

entomology textbook I found that these very small dark brown to black flies are freeloader flies in the family Milichiidae.

After yet more research I found little specific information on them but generally speaking many are kleptoparasites, making their living by stealing food from other diners.

So how could these tiny flies find such a recently killed bee? There are at least two possibilities. Kleptoparasitic flies may rely on olfaction, like vultures that can detect dead animal odors from long distances. But in some cases, a freeloader fly has been observed riding on a crab spider, possibly waiting for the predator to make a kill.

A Winter Hideaway for Bird Droppings?

Have you ever wondered how caterpillars spend the winter? For one species, an artisan-built home complete with a sun deck, of

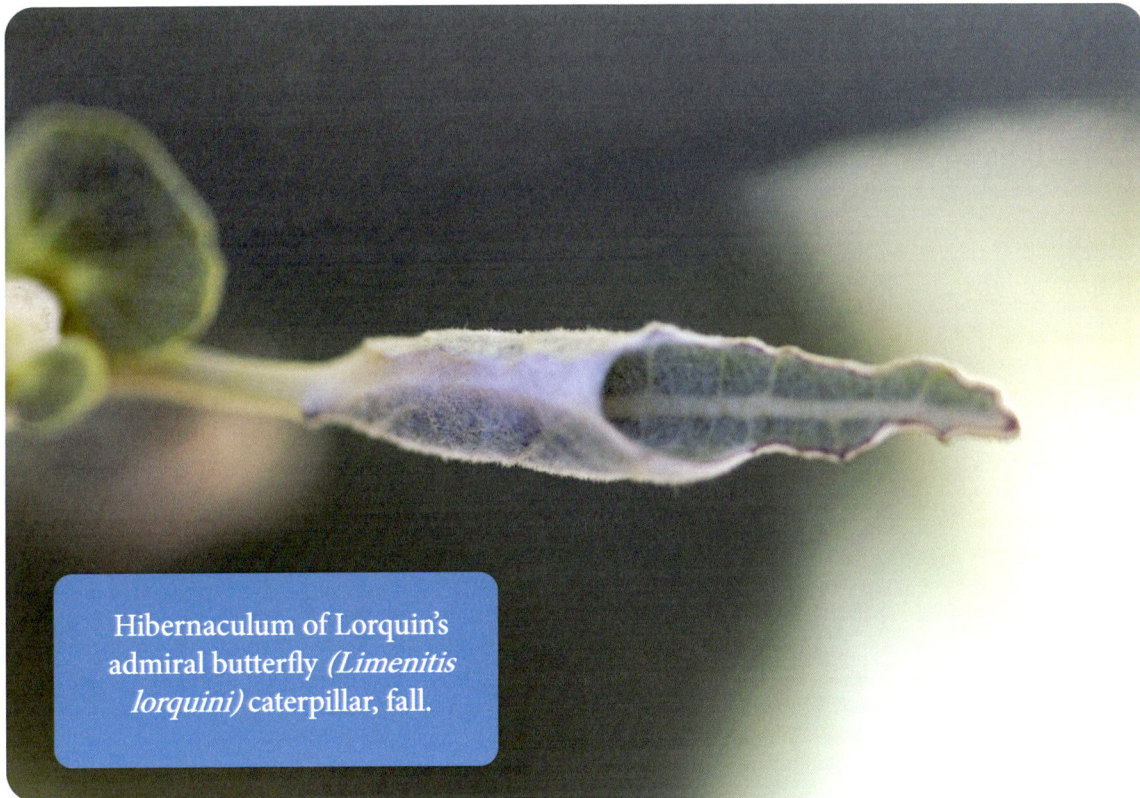

Hibernaculum of Lorquin's admiral butterfly *(Limenitis lorquini)* caterpillar, fall.

Hibernaculum of Lorquin's admiral butterfly caterpillar, late winter. Note the "thorny" caterpillar guarding the entrance.

course. Meet Lorquin's admiral butterfly *(Limenitis lorquini)*. This common butterfly occurs throughout the Pacific Northwest from British Columbia to southern California.

The female Lorquin's lays her eggs on the upper surface of cherry or willow leaves in late summer. When the caterpillar hatches, it feeds on the leaves but doesn't grow much in size. In the fall, as the leaves are yellowing and starting to fall from the host plant, the caterpillar chooses a leaf for its winter home, or hibernaculum, and produces silk threads to attach the leaf's stem solidly to the tree branch. With the leaf secured, the caterpillar cuts out a small piece of leaf along the stem and midvein as the base of the hibernaculum. The next phase of home construction is to silk the two long sides of the leaf together to form a tube, leaving the end with a wide opening so that the winter hideaway strongly resembles an empty cornucopia.

For the next five to six months this will be the caterpillar's home through rain, wind, snow, and the dangers of bird predation. On sunny winter days, it will lounge on its sun deck, the wide lower shelf of the cornucopia.

Another bird dropping mimic: Lorquin's admiral butterfly caterpillar feeding on willow leaves.

While I have found no documentation on why the larva sunbathes (thus exposing itself to predators), I suspect that the winter sunshine benefits the caterpillar in some way--much as humans produce vitamin D from sun exposure. Simply warming up the caterpillar doesn't seem to be the purpose because it has no food to eat to support energy use.

With the arrival of spring, the caterpillar leaves its hibernaculum to dine on new leaves. Its appearance changes dramatically from small and dark brown to big and brown with a huge splash of white blanketing large parts of its body, so that it looks like a splotch of fresh bird poop (the white splotch even looks damp, though it is not). The caterpillar's head is now covered in spines, with a pair of large clubs also covered in spines. To complete the bird-poop mimicry, midway down its back are a pair of dorsal bumps that look just like undigested berry seeds sticking out of the bird droppings. It's the little details that count!

I found and photographed an overwintering Lorquin's caterpillar and its hibernaculum on a willow tree in my garden one year. All winter, I kept my fingers crossed for the caterpillar's survival, since chestnut-backed chickadees

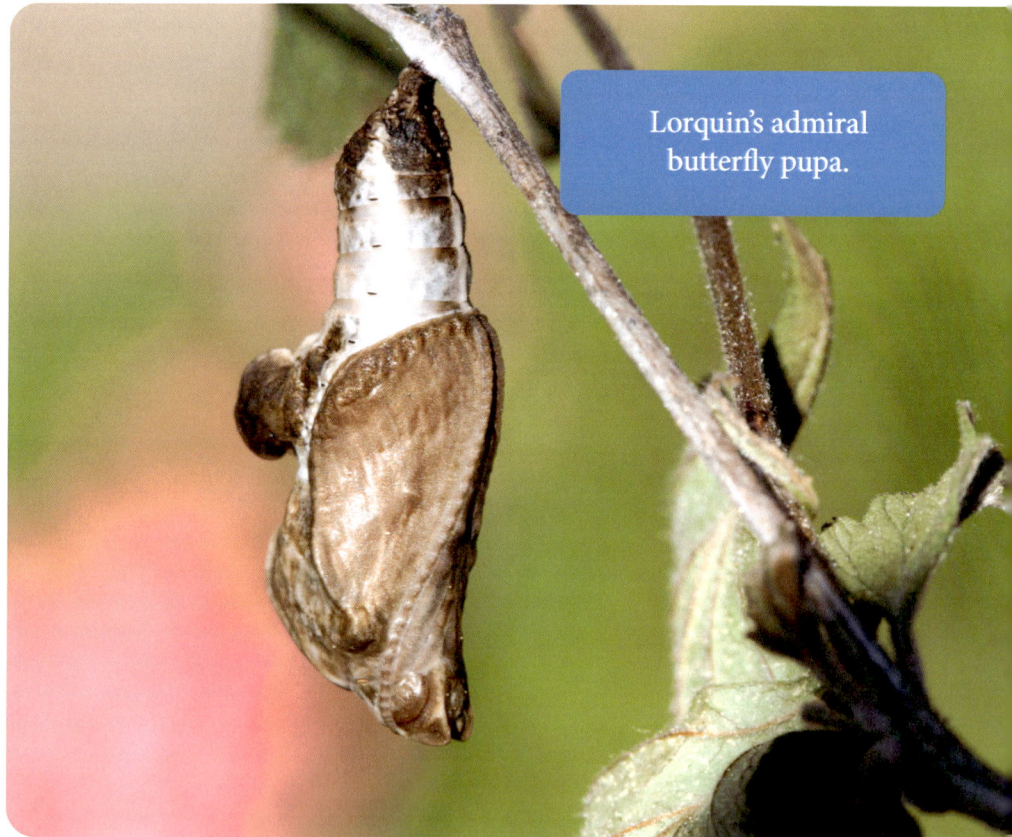

Lorquin's admiral butterfly pupa.

(Poecile rufescens) regularly hunted insects on the willow tree. The caterpillar made it through winter, and then spring, and finally emerged from pupation as a beautiful butterfly.

The Galls

Would you believe that a tiny insect can control the chemical and biological functions of a tree? It may even be happening in your own garden. Various species of insects can cause trees and other plants to produce abnormal tissue growths known as galls. Some wasps and flies can even induce plants to produce galls of a certain shape or color, move nutrients around the plant to benefit the insect, and concentrate plant tannins in the gall's outer cells to protect it from other plant-feeding animals.

The main purpose of most galls is to provide food and a protective home for

Lorquin's admiral butterfly adult.

The gall midge (genus *Iteomyia*) causes willow tooth galls to grow on willow leaves.

you will find a single tiny sawfly larva. Once the larva reaches maturity, it chews a hole in the gall and drops to the ground, where it pupates before emerging in the spring as an adult.

Another common gall in urban/suburban

Willow apple sawfly *(Pontania californica)* galls; herbivorous insects like these green-and-black sawfly larvae feed on the leaf but not on the chemically protected galls.

the insect's larvae. Plant galls may appear on buds, leaves, stems, flowers, or roots. In the urban/ suburban garden, willow leaves are particularly rich in insect-induced galls. Willow apple gall is caused by a wasp-sawfly *(Pontania californica)* and is one of the most common and easily observable galls. The gall forms a shiny round "apple" about ten to twelve millimeters in diameter, red on the leaf's upper surface and yellow-green on its underside. If you cut into the gall

landscapes is willow tooth gall, caused by midges and other small flies in the genus *Iteomyia*. Clumps of galls project from the bottom of the willow leaf and resemble a pale green molar. The upper surface is flat and smooth. Each gall contains a single midge larva; the larva and leaf drop to the ground in the fall and the adult midge emerges from pupation in the spring.

In this chapter, I have given you a glimpse into the complex lives of a few animals that might already be living in your yard. If they are not, do your best to encourage them to move in!

Spiny rose gall *(Diplolepis bicolor)* enhancing the beauty of this native rose.

CONCLUSION: SOD HOUSES   8

When my mother was a young girl, she lived in a flat treeless part of North Dakota where sod was the most readily available building material and buffalo chips were the cheapest fuel for heating. The land around the isolated farmsteads provided the only resources that people had access to. Food came from gardens, cultivated fields, livestock, and wild lands. For Native Americans and European settlers, utter reliance on the local landscape was the only possible way of life.

Now, in the twenty-first century, we are relearning that lesson: we are entirely reliant on this earth . . . a healthy earth.

What can we do to help restore the health of our planet? Start with things we can control locally. Remove your lawn and rewild your

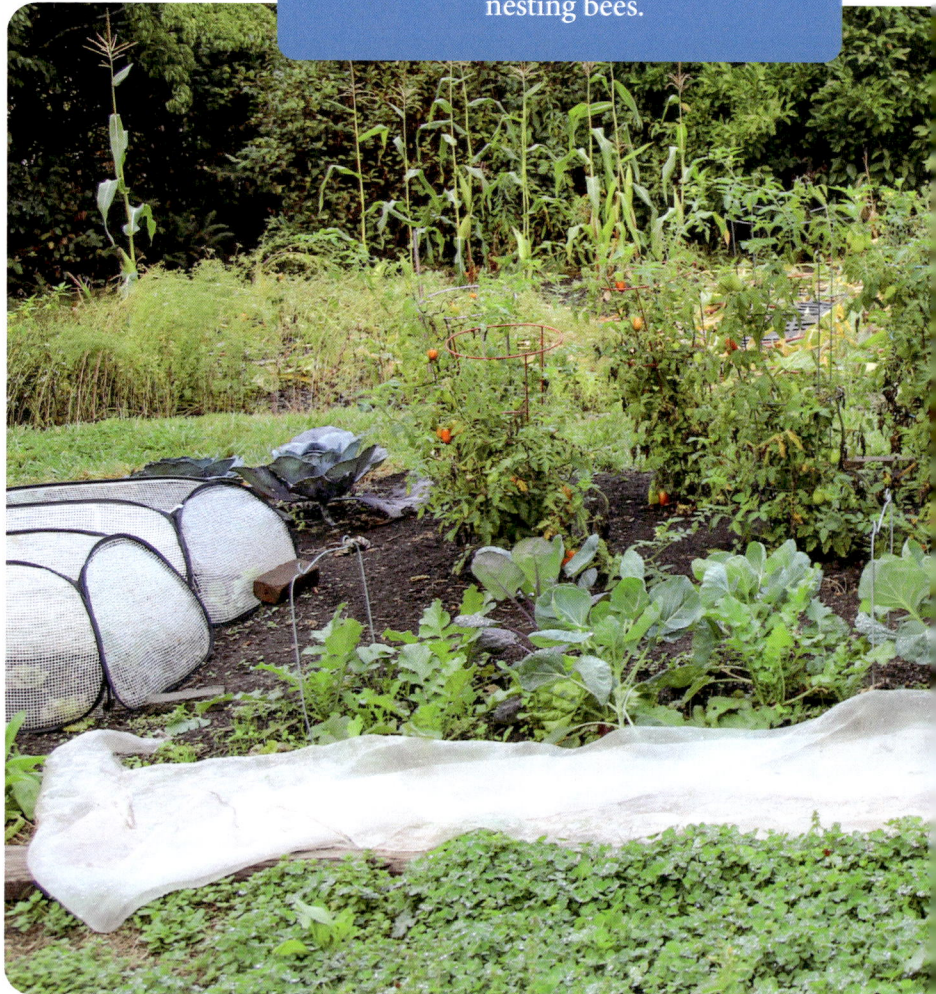

Vegetable gardening provides you with food and a direct connection to nature's rhythms. Bare soil around vegetables can be important habitat for ground nesting bees.

yard with the original native plants that attract endemic wildlife and increase biodiversity. Advocate for more natural areas, parks, and community gardens in urban areas. Encourage municipalities to plant wildlife friendly native plants, which will help provide food and habitat for wild animals affected by urban expansion. Volunteer to help plant native plants in a city park.

Like the early farmers who used sod houses carved from the prairie soil to survive in a very harsh environment, and like the Indigenous peoples who lived in balance with the land, we can use a connection with nature to try to regain a sense of its importance. As you rewild your yard with the help of this book, you will help native wildlife to survive in urban and suburban areas. As you plant, care for, and harvest a food garden, you will experience a direct dependence on climate, soil, and weather, connecting you directly to the land and making you an active land steward.

For my mother, living in rhythm with nature and the changing seasons was her only option. For you and me, getting back in touch with that rhythm can bring endless benefits, not only for ourselves but for the Earth itself.

Native plant garden that provides food and habitat for wildlife.

INDEX:

western tiger swallowtail butterfly *Papilio rutulus* 32c, 52c, 71, 72c, 73, 132-133, 132c, 133c

western toad *Anaxyrus boreas* 41-42, 43c, 44, 110, 123, 123c, 124c, 125-127, 125c, 126c

western yellowjacket *Vespula pensylvanica* 29, 32c, 66, 91

white-crowned sparrow *Zonotrichia leucophrys* 12c

white-lined sphinx moth *Hyles lineata* 71, 75, 75c

wild onion *Allium* 3c

willow apple gall *Pontania californica* 140-141, 140c

willow leaf beetle *Chrysomela aeneicollis* 11c

willow *Salix* 9, 18-19, 21c, 47, 58, 66, 73, 106, 137-141

willow tooth gall *Iteomyia* 140c, 141

wind 11, 14-15, 103, 105

wood/bark pile 57, 108c, 111, 112c

woodpecker 5c, 20, 22-23c, 47

woolly bear (Erebidae) 122c, 127-128, 127c, 128c, 129c, 131

yellow-faced bumble bee *Bombus vosnesenskii* 57c

yellow-spotted tiger moth *Lophocampa maculata* 127c, 128

yellow-spotted/cyanide millipede *Harpaphe haydeniana* 131c, 132

zebra jumping spider *Salticus scenicus* 38-39, 39c

www.ingramcontent.com/pod-product-compliance
Lightning Source LLC
Chambersburg PA
CBRC101142030426
42335CB00008B/205

9781962081252